HBR Guide to
Beating
Burnout

Harvard Business Review Guides

Arm yourself with the advice you need to succeed on the job, from the most trusted brand in business. Packed with how-to essentials from leading experts, the HBR Guides provide smart answers to your most pressing work challenges.

The titles include:

HBR Guide for Women at Work

HBR Guide to Being More Productive

HBR Guide to Better Business Writing

HBR Guide to Building Your Business Case

HBR Guide to Buying a Small Business

HBR Guide to Changing Your Career

HBR Guide to Coaching Employees

HBR Guide to Data Analytics Basics for Managers

HBR Guide to Dealing with Conflict

HBR Guide to Delivering Effective Feedback

HBR Guide to Emotional Intelligence

HBR Guide to Finance Basics for Managers

HBR Guide to Getting the Mentoring You Need

HBR Guide to Getting the Right Work Done

HBR Guide to Leading Teams

HBR Guide to Making Better Decisions

HBR Guide to Making Every Meeting Matter

HBR Guide to Managing Strategic Initiatives

HBR Guide to Managing Stress at Work

HBR Guide to
Beating
Burnout

HARVARD BUSINESS REVIEW PRESS

Boston, Massachusetts

Copyright 2021 Harvard Business School Publishing Corporation

All rights reserved

Printed in the United States of America

10 9 8 7 6 5 4 3 2 1

No part of this publication may be reproduced, stored in or introduced into a retrieval system, or transmitted, in any form, or by any means (electronic, mechanical, photocopying, recording, or otherwise), without the prior permission of the publisher. Requests for permission should be directed to permissions@harvardbusiness.org, or mailed to Permissions, Harvard Business School Publishing, 60 Harvard Way, Boston, Massachusetts 02163.

The web addresses referenced in this book were live and correct at the time of the book's publication but may be subject to change.

Library of Congress Cataloging-in-Publication Data

Names: Harvard Business Review Press.
Title: HBR guide to beating burnout.
Other titles: Harvard Business Review guide to beating burnout |
    Harvard business review guides.
Description: Boston, Massachusetts : Harvard Business Review Press,
    [2020] | Series: HBR guides | Includes index.
Identifiers: LCCN 2020026107 (print) | LCCN 2020026108 (ebook) |
    ISBN 9781647820008 (paperback) | ISBN 9781647820015 (ebook)
Subjects: LCSH: Burn out (Psychology) | Leadership. | Industrial
    management.
Classification: LCC BF481 .H398 2020 (print) | LCC BF481 (ebook) |
    DDC 158.7/23—dc23
LC record available at https://lccn.loc.gov/2020026107
LC ebook record available at https://lccn.loc.gov/2020026108

ISBN: 978-1-64782-000-8
eISBN: 978-1-64782-001-5

The paper used in this publication meets the requirements of the American National Standard for Permanence of Paper for Publications and Documents in Libraries and Archives Z39.48-1992.

What You'll Learn

It's a fact of professional life that you'll need to deal with stress and overwork, but we can handle only so much of each before we risk burning out. The personal and professional consequences of burnout are debilitating: You feel as if you're in a fog of exhaustion, negativity, and ineffectiveness. You feel disillusioned with your job, and your productivity slows to a crawl. Your work, home life, and health all suffer.

Fortunately, there are steps you can take to prevent and recover from burnout. This book will help you understand the causes and risk factors, how to protect yourself and your team, and what you should do now if you're already suffering from burnout.

One of the most common myths about burnout is that it's a work-life balance problem, not a workplace problem. But we shouldn't try to take on burnout by ourselves; real change needs to happen at the team and organizational levels. No matter your role in your company, you can make a difference. Set reasonable and healthy expectations for yourself and others. Be aware of signs of burnout in your employees and coworkers. Design jobs and make hires that will push back against burnout culture. Together with your colleagues, you can combat burnout and make your workplace more psychologically safe and productive.

This guide contains practical tips and advice to help you and your team navigate the perils of workplace burnout. You'll learn how to:

- Assess your level of risk

- Distinguish between stress and burnout

- Recognize the symptoms in yourself and others

- Mitigate the effects of always-on culture when working at home

- Understand how passion can lead to burnout

- Return to healthy engagement

- Know when you need to leave your job

- Prevent burnout on your team—even if *you're* burned out

- Protect your high performers from burning out

- Assess and measure levels of burnout in your organization

- Contribute to a happier, healthier workplace of the future

Contents

Contents

SECTION TWO

Bouncing Back from Burnout

SECTION THREE

Preventing Burnout on Your Team

Contents

SECTION FOUR

How Organizations Can Combat Burnout

Rethinking Burnout

by Jennifer Moss

For over 40 years, scientists, academics, and workplace experts were stuck in debate over a clear, unified definition of "burnout." While the discussion dragged on, popular culture defined it for us. We were told that burnout is a work-life balance problem, not a workplace problem, a "me" issue, not a "we" issue. We were ushered down the path of trying to solve burnout by ourselves, struggling to fix a problem that wasn't ours alone to fix.

Finally, in 2019, the World Health Organization (WHO) attempted to put an end to the debate by including burnout in the 11th revision of the International Classification of Diseases (ICD-11) as an occupational phenomenon, a "syndrome conceptualized as resulting from chronic *workplace* stress that has not been successfully managed." Although the WHO didn't clearly state that accountability should reside at the organizational level, it placed a stake firmly in the ground by claiming burnout "refers specifically to phenomena in the *occupational* context and should not be applied to describe experiences in other areas of life" (italics in both quotes are mine).

This is a big deal. For decades, we had to preface the syndrome as "occupational burnout." Now that the WHO has clearly demarcated burnout as a workplace problem, organizations are on notice. Leaders must focus on systems and policies that prioritize psychological safety for their employees, as they do for physical safety. We have clear rules that protect people from working in smoke-filled spaces or buildings riddled with asbestos; shouldn't we equally protect them from working in emotionally toxic environments that systemically cause burnout?

How to Detect Something We Cannot See

Three of the foremost experts on burnout—Christina Maslach, Michael Leiter, and Susan E. Jackson—agree that burnout is an occupational phenomenon. In 1981, the team was responsible for developing the Maslach Burnout Inventory (MBI), an assessment intended to help organizations gather data to better navigate the unknowns of burnout. Forty years later, their findings would become the basis for the WHO announcement.

Maslach, Leiter, and Jackson defined burnout as a "psychological syndrome emerging as a prolonged response to chronic interpersonal stressors on the job. The three key dimensions of this response are overwhelming exhaustion, feelings of cynicism and detachment from the job, and a sense of ineffectiveness and lack of accomplishment." Although these three dimensions—*exhaustion*, *cynicism*, and *professional efficacy*—helped us understand the negative outcomes of burnout, it remained a challenge to reliably detect them in ourselves and others.

As the MBI has evolved through four editions, it continues to be the best benchmark for measuring burnout and the strongest defense against it, when its results are interpreted properly. However, leaders often struggle to administer the MBI correctly or interpret the MBI's findings, rendering their best weapon as useless or even harmful. (Maslach and Leiter discuss these misuses and explain how organizations can avoid them in chapter 24 of this guide.)

Burnout may also hide in the data when leaders look to measures like engagement and productivity as yardsticks for well-being, which often grossly misdiagnose underlying issues like stress, anxiety, and subsequently burnout. High performers are excellent at meeting productivity goals and often self-report as engaged even when they are highly stressed and burned out. Researchers at Plasticity Labs conducted a study that analyzed 3,500 educational professionals over three years and found that in all roles, engagement was high.[1] For years, leaders had used this measure as the foundation for their strategic wellness programming and resource allocations. Only when the researchers started to gather data specific to well-being and other social-emotional factors like hope, efficacy, resilience, stress, and overall happiness levels, did they realize that although employees were engaged, many were burned out and significantly unwell.

To detect the things we cannot see, we have to ask better questions further upstream. A simple yet powerful question is to ask your employees, "What is the single biggest frustration you are experiencing right now?" Typically, the problems are just small, irritating, daily experiences that chip away at people. They are the broken-down printers at the nurses' station that force staff to run down the hall to the working printer for their patients' printouts—despite the $100 cost for repair. They show up in coffee you have to pay for in the break room because "times are tight." They appear when "working from home" means you have to post to Slack every time you take a five-minute break. They appear in excruciating ways, as when an email pops up from your boss at 10:00 p.m. with a not-so-subtle expectation for a response. They are the bathroom stalls where you have to pump your breast milk because there is no other private place. They are the empty parking spots you drive past, reserved for VIPs who never use them, and the exorbitant budgets for things you can never use.

These few examples are all preventable; yet if there are no mechanisms to monitor issues like these—or anyone asking the staff what is gnawing at them—they end up being like a sickness that festers and spreads.

Burnout can be detected. We can see the unseen. It just requires an intentional and frequent interest in how people are feeling and a commitment to follow through. It also helps to identify which groups are at the highest risk.

Caregiver Syndrome and Passion-Driven Burnout

The Mayo Clinic describes the list of job burnout risk factors as:

- You identify so strongly with work that you lack balance between your work life and your personal life

- You have a high workload, including overtime work

- You try to be everything to everyone

- You work in a helping profession, such as health care

- You feel you have little or no control over your work

- Your job is monotonous[2]

While burnout can affect anyone, at any age, in any industry, there are certain sectors and roles at increased risk. Purpose-driven work—work people love and feel passionately about—is one of them. Mission-driven executives, nonprofit employees, teachers, principals, nurses, and physicians are some of the people most at risk for burnout. According to a study published in the *Journal of Personality,* this type of labor can breed obsessive passion (as opposed to harmonious passion), which predicts an increase of conflict and, thus, burnout.[3] On its list, the Mayo Clinic attributes several risks—the first, third, and fourth items—to caregiver and passion-driven burnout.

Notably however, anyone passionate about what they do is at high risk of burnout, especially high performers. A Canadian study analyzed responses from 3,715 employees across 12 organizations and found that employees driven by purpose are significantly more stressed and score lower for well-being, resilience, and self-efficacy than those who are not. David Whiteside, who has a PhD in organizational behavior and led the study, emphasized that "despite the clear benefits of feeling meaningfully connected to your work, our data suggests that there are often real and undiscussed complications of purpose-driven work on employees' health that can be related to the experience of burnout long-term."[4]

The Effects of a Pandemic on the Burnout Epidemic

Burnout almost always stems from three unsustainable workplace practices: untenable workload, misalignment with the values of the organization, or routine overqualification for a job. Each of these begins at work and spills over into life outside work; well-being doesn't bifurcate between nine-to-five work and home. If work is the cause of our stress and anxiety and is causing us to burn out, we feel it in every area of our lives.

So, when a massive event like the global Covid-19 pandemic disrupts the workforce at epic proportions, we feel the effects of collective burnout at an entirely new level. Roger McIntyre, University of Toronto professor of psychiatry and pharmacology, has described the acceleration of burnout as an "echo pandemic."

Long before the chaos of Covid-19, burnout was a rapidly evolving epidemic of its own. According to Stanford University researchers in 2016, the effects of workplace stress totaled $190 billion in the United States every year—roughly 8% of national health-care outlays—and resulted in 120,000 deaths.[5] Worldwide, 615 million suffer from depression and anxiety, which, according to a recent WHO study, cost the global workforce an estimated $1 trillion in lost productivity each year. The years ahead are sure to push these numbers to even more alarming levels.

Amid the pandemic, far too many people risked their personal safety to bring critical services to the public. These essential workers were offered salary raises, only to have them clawed back when it was deemed safe to be at work. Health-care workers were required to jump into a war zone each day, battling at the front lines without adequate equipment, tools, resources, and breaks. Within a few months of the outbreak, 47% of Canadian health-care workers reported a need for psychological support. In China, the workers reported high rates of depression (50%), anxiety (45%), and insomnia (34%). And in Pakistan, large numbers reported moderate (42%) to severe (26%) psychological distress.[6] After days filled with death and enormous personal risk, health-care workers would go home to quarantine, waving to their spouses and children when they most needed a hug.

We may not fully grasp the impact of the pandemic on the workforce for years, but there is no denying that the major shifts in how we work are certain to cause burnout if ignored. Collective stress and anxiety skyrocketed to its highest levels in decades. Not only were people concerned for their health, but many were suddenly thrust into a steep remote-work learning curve, forced to add 30% more hours just to reach the same pre-pandemic productivity levels. Multiply this by the roughly 2.6 billion people in lockdown worldwide at the height of the pandemic.

The additional stresses brought on by the crisis hit at-risk populations all the more sharply. According to research by Adia Harvey Wingfield, professor of arts and sciences and associate dean at Washington University, Black health-care providers are subject to a specific kind of burnout, stress, and exhaustion: "Frequently, this happens not only because many are working in under-resourced public facilities, but because they are also dealing with the racial implications of their work—caring for low-income patients of color whom even many of their white colleagues view through a racially stereotyped lens as drug abusers, noncompliant patients, or irresponsible parents."[7]

Another important voice on the topic of Black burnout is award-winning author and poet Tiana Clark, who teaches creative writing at Southern Illinois University at Edwardsville. In response to a piece on millennial burnout that omitted the Black experience of burnout, she wrote that when it comes to burnout for Black Americans, "the data is bleak." Getting paid 61 cents for every dollar a white male counterpart makes is already disturbingly unjust, but compounded with the stress of the everyday racism the Black workforce experiences, it is exhausting. Clark says, "Burnout for white, upper-middle-class millennials might be taxing mentally, but the consequences of being overworked and underpaid while managing microaggressions toward marginalized groups damages our bodies by the minute with greater intensity."[8]

We need to make sure the questions we ask about burnout are nuanced and inclusive. If we gather data with bias, we get data that doesn't serve everyone—and a one-size-fits-all approach to battling burnout.

Another at-risk group for burnout is working parents, especially as the number of families in which both parents worked outside the home doubled over the last 30 years.[9] Already pulled in too many directions, by and large the pandemic overwhelmed them. Attempting to work full-time while homeschooling their children and keeping them safe amid uncertainty and social isolation was literally exhausting. Early research from the lockdown claimed that 46% of parents stated their stress level was 8 or greater (out of 10), and 28% of quarantined parents warranted a diagnosis of "trauma-related mental health disorder."[10]

On a more optimistic note, working from home and having flexible work hours are positives for many employees and their employers. One Stanford study, led by professor Nicholas Bloom, analyzed 500 employees who were divided into two groups, with half working at home and the other half remaining in the office.[11] The outcomes sided significantly in favor of working from home. In this group, employee attrition was reduced by 50 percent among the virtual employees, and they took shorter breaks, took less time off, and had fewer sick days. The company also saved approximately $2,000 per employee on commercial rent.

Work from Home Forever . . . Cause or Cure?

Another major shift as a result of lockdown was the number of people who would choose to work from home indefinitely. It kicked off a wave of companies going "digital first," where suddenly offices were shuttered. While a significant portion of the knowledge-based workforce has long sought this kind of flexibility (a large-scale poll of people in multiple industries found that 59% say they would happily stay working from home, given the option); others were loath to give up face-to-face meetings, high-fives, handshakes, and a defined barrier between work and home.[12]

Industries like tech were mostly thrilled by the new policy. Teachers felt the opposite, many describing virtual learning as a failed experiment. Stories of educators (both a helping profession and a passion profession) leaving their field because of burnout were rampant on social media and in the news cycle.[13] According to one survey of 8,100 teachers and school leaders, up to 70% felt "exhausted and disconnected from students, with some losing sleep over learning struggles and some students' inability to adapt to remote learning."[14]

And despite the enthusiasm for the work-from-home future, when we dig into the data during the pandemic, employees were working an average of three more hours per day to achieve the same productivity results, and women were adding an extra 20 hours per week as they were the primary jugglers of family and work at home. Remote employees require specialized management; employers need to watch for signs of burnout within ourselves and employees. Simply analyzing productivity levels is not enough for leaders to determine whether this policy is truly sustainable.

Business as Unusual

Adjusting to such a major disruption in our workforce and in our lives will take years; we may never go back to business as usual. Although change can conjure feelings of anxiety and uncertainty, it can also give us huge opportunities for growth, depending on how we use adversity to our benefit. States of discomfort often force us to find new footing, and if there was ever a time of discomfort, 2020 was it. Addressing topics of well-being, mental health, and mental illness has never been more paramount. As we've witnessed the pervasive stress and peered deeply into our colleagues' lives via webcam, we can't, as employers, deny our role and responsibility in employees' overall well-being. This change gives us a wide berth to tackle burnout where we can—for ourselves, our teams, and our organizations—and to make it a strategic priority.

As you navigate through the four sections of the guide, think about what we've experienced collectively. We have jointly gone through an event that was transformative—because of its global nature and our access to information—unlike any other experience in history. This was no small feat, but people worldwide rose up together. As you read the work of brilliant scientists, scholars, and experts, imagine how you can rethink burnout for a healthier, happier, post-pandemic future at work. How can we take this collective compassion and empathy and make it fuel for driving change? And, if we were willing to make all the sacrifices to protect strangers in our community, why wouldn't we make an equal effort in our workplaces? Because when it comes to burnout, lives hang in the balance—possibly your own. The time to get it right is now.

―――――――

Jennifer Moss is an award-winning journalist, author, and international public speaker. She is a CBC Radio columnist, reporting on topics related to happiness and well-being. She contributes regularly to *Harvard Business Review* and writes for the Society of Human Resource Management (SHRM). She sits on the Global Happiness Council in support of the UN's Sustainable Development Goals related to well-being. Her book *Unlocking Happiness at Work* was named Business Book of the Year, and her forthcoming book on burnout will be published by Harvard Business Review Press.

NOTES

1. "Employee Well-Being, Productivity, and Firm Performance: Evidence and Case Studies," *Global Happiness Policy Report 2019*, Appendix B, https://s3.amazonaws.com/ghwbpr-2019/GH19_Ch5A_Appendix.pdf.

2. Mayo Clinic, "Job Burnout: How to Spot It and Take Action," November 21, 2018, https://www.mayoclinic.org/healthy-lifestyle/adult-health/in-depth/burnout/art-20046642.

3. Geneviève A. Mangeau, Robert J. Vallerand, Julie Charest, Sarah-Jane Salvy, Nathalie Lacaille, Thérèse Bouffard, and Richard

Koestner, "On the Development of Harmonious and Obsessive Passion: The Role of Autonomy Support, Activity Specialization, and Identification with the Activity," *Journal of Personality* 77, no. 3 (June 2009): 601–646.

4. Dave Whiteside (website), "The Anatomy of a Purpose-Driven Employee," https://www.davewhiteside.com/anatomyofapurpose drivenemployee.

5. Joel Goh, Jeffrey Pfeffer, and Stefanos Zenios, "The Relationship Between Workplace Stressors and Mortality and Health Costs in the United States," *Management Science* 62, no. 2 (2016): 608–628.

6. "Covid-19 and the Need for Action on Mental Health," *United Nations Policy Brief*, May 13, 2020, https://www.un.org/sites/un2.un .org/files/un_policy_brief-covid_and_mental_health_final.pdf.

7. Adia Harvey Wingfield, "The Disproportionate Impact of Covid-19 on Black Health Care Workers in the U.S.," *Harvard Business Review*, May 2020.

8. Tiana Clark, "This Is What Black Burnout Feels Like," *BuzzFeed News*, January 11, 2019, https://www.buzzfeednews.com/article/ tianaclarkpoet/millennial-burnout-black-women-self-care-anxiety -depression.

9. Sharanjit Uppal, "Employment Patterns of Families with Children," *Insights on Canadian Society*, May 25, 2020, https://www150 .statcan.gc.ca/n1/pub/75-006-x/2015001/article/14202-eng.htm.

10. Elke Van Hoof, "Lockdown Is the World's Biggest Psychological Experiment—And We Will Pay the Price," World Economic Forum, April 9, 2020, https://www.weforum.org/agenda/2020/04/this-is-the -psychological-side-of-the-covid-19-pandemic-that-were-ignoring/.

11. Nicholas Bloom, James Liang, John Roberts, and Zhichun Jenny Ying, "Does Working from Home Work? Evidence from a Chinese Experiment," *The Quarterly Journal of Economics* (2015): 165–218.

12. "Working from Home Perceptions," Pulse, May 19, 2020, https://fluentpulse.com/covid-19-working-from-home/.

13. Laura Hensley, "'It Breaks You': Teacher Goes Viral with Post About Why She Quit Her Job," *Global News*, June 21, 2019, https:// globalnews.ca/news/5416313/teaching-stress-viral-post-burnout/.

14. "Alberta Teachers Responding to Coronavirus (COVID-19)— Pandemic Research Survey Study," Alberta Teachers' Association, n.d., https://www.teachers.ab.ca/News%20Room/Issues/COVID-19/ Pages/Covid-19-Survey.aspx.

Protecting Yourself from Burnout

CHAPTER 1

Don't Get Surprised by Burnout

by Steven D'Souza

Coming back to the U.K. after an intensive, three-day consulting trip, I was on the edge of a panic attack. For a few seconds, I had a vivid "day-mare" of myself in the hospital, surrounded by doctors, with no way to cope or communicate coherently. As the vision passed, I became aware, for the first time in a long time, of a great heaviness and tiredness in my body. I realized—with some surprise—that I was burned out.

Adapted from content posted on hbr.org, June 17, 2016 (product #H02XIL).

On the back of an envelope, I calculated that I had been working in over a dozen countries during the last few months—sometimes three countries in a single week. Because my collaborators and clients span time zones, the days were often long. Maybe I should have seen this coming.

It's not as if there were no warning signs. Some of these were pretty big: I'd had writer's block for months, seemingly unable to start my new book. Some were smaller but no less telltale: It took me five weeks on an assignment in Singapore to even realize the hotel over-looked a beach!

Why was I so oblivious to being on the edge of burn-out—or, more accurately, descending further into burn-out? Perhaps because I love my work and often don't frame it as work. If this is a problem, I reasoned, it's one lots of people would love to have. I feel very lucky to do work I am passionate about, and I like the people I get to work with.

And yet such positivity, I've learned, can backfire. Because I love and appreciate my work, my mental "im-mune system" had nothing to reject. It had become too much of a good thing; the axiom "a strength overplayed can be a liability" leaps to mind.

Here's the tricky part. Therapy, coaching, exercise, or meditation may relieve the symptoms of burnout and help us cope—or even thrive—in these conditions, but they won't necessarily change the conditions themselves.

For those of us who have already tried mindfulness and deep breathing and other exercises, and are still struggling with burnout, we might also need to challenge some fundamental assumptions around how much we can really do and develop the capability and permission to not do.

We don't have the capacity to "do it all," just as we cannot "have it all."

In a world of excess doing, we need to develop the capacity to mindfully choose not to do. This is far from easy, as it means confronting deeply held beliefs, many cultural as well as personal, that have served us well to date: "Time is money." "If it's not done perfectly, it isn't worth doing." Even the tyranny of the seemingly positive "Carpe Diem" in which we must make every moment count.

At what cost? The truth is, we are much more fragile than we think. We need moments of not doing; we need moments that don't count. It's these moments that spur creativity and productivity when we turn back to "doing" mode.

For example, with my writer's block in full swing and our new book completely stalled, my coauthors and I had a meeting where we shared our frustration at our lack of progress. Frankly, I was wondering whether to abandon the project altogether and be done with the feelings of guilt and shame for not contributing. We decided that, rather than push ahead with more commitments and more check-in dates, we would give ourselves permission not to do anything, just for a few weeks. Just to notice and be with our own thoughts, curiosities, and preoccupations, accepting where we were. Paradoxically, it was at this moment that suddenly I found myself full of ideas and eager to put them down on paper.

In busy organizational lives, with deadlines to meet and clients to serve, "permission not to do" is far more subtle and needs to be negotiated with others. As I've tried to make peace with not doing, there are three things that have helped me:

Becoming More Aware of "Close Enemies"

Close enemies is a Buddhist concept that describes two things that sound very similar but produce opposite results. For example, it might be "endurance" and "resilience." They sound closely related, but an executive working on endurance may find themselves feeling more and more depleted as they try to do more and more. If you're focused on building resilience, however, you ought to feel replenished. Notice which activities genuinely replenish you, and which are simply another thing to get done.

Welcoming Gaps as Opportunities to Rest, Not Inconveniences

When caught up in the pressure to do, we are often hyperaware of all the gaps in our day: waiting in a queue or commuting. To a doer, the inefficiency of these gaps can feel frustrating, so we check our mobiles while we wait, or schedule calls for our commutes. But if we're comfortable with not doing, we can take these as opportunities not to do, but to rest.

Instead of pulling out your phone, just try breathing in and out, making the out-breath twice as long as the in-breath. As you breathe, rest in the tiny space between the out-breath and the in-breath, then start the process again when you need to take an in-breath. Coming back to the breath and body produces what Dr. Herbert Benson, Harvard Medical School, calls the "relaxation response" and calms the nervous system.

Creating a "Not Do" List

A "not do" list includes behaviors you know are not helpful for you. You might include not spending time on social media in the evening, or not checking your phone while talking with your family or loved ones. You can also list tasks you plan to outsource or delegate, or work tasks that you will do—eventually—just not today. This has helped me feel less guilty about whatever it is I'm not doing and has helped me focus more wholeheartedly on the task in front of me. Share your not-do list with close friends or colleagues you trust to build accountability and support.

Steven D'Souza is the director of Deeper Learning Ltd., an associate professor at IE Business School, Madrid, and associate fellow of the Saïd Business School, University of Oxford. He is the author or coauthor of *Made in Britain* with Patrick Clarke, *Brilliant Networking*, and *Not Knowing* with Diana Renner, which won the CMI Management Book of the Year, and *Not Doing* with Diana Renner. He is listed on the Thinkers 50 Radar and *HR Magazine*'s "Most Influential" list. He is working on a forthcoming book with Diana Renner and Robert Poynton. Follow him on Twitter @stevenxdsouza.

CHAPTER 2

Six Causes of Burnout, and How to Avoid Them

by Elizabeth Grace Saunders

You know you're on the verge of burnout: You're perpetually exhausted, annoyed, and feeling unaccomplished and unappreciated. Everything in you wants to quit your job. But is that the best choice? Ultimately only you can know what is right in your situation. But there is research that can help you determine whether you can salvage your current job or whether the mismatch between you and your current position is so great that you need to look for a new one.

Adapted from content posted on hbr.org, July 5, 2019 (product #H0518G).

Various models help to explain and predict burnout. One, called the Areas of Worklife model (drawn from research by Christina Maslach and Michael P. Leiter of the University of California at Berkeley and Acadia University, respectively) identifies six areas where you could experience imbalances that lead to burnout. As a time management coach, I've seen that some individuals can make positive shifts in one or more of these areas and then happily stay in their current position, while others discover that the mismatch is still too great and decide that it's time to move on.

Here are the six areas that can lead to burnout and how you can attempt to remedy each one.

1. Workload

When you have a workload that matches your capacity, you can effectively get your work done, have opportunities for rest and recovery, and find time for professional growth and development. When you chronically feel overloaded, these opportunities to restore balance don't exist.

To address the stress of your workload, assess how well you're doing in these key areas: planning your workload, prioritizing your work, delegating tasks, saying no, and letting go of perfectionism. If you haven't been doing one or more of these things, try to make progress in these time management skill areas and then see how you feel. For many individuals, especially those who have a bent toward people pleasing, some proactive effort on reducing their workload can significantly reduce feelings of burnout and provide space to rest.

2. Perceived Lack of Control

Feeling as if you lack autonomy, access to resources, and a say in decisions that impact your professional life can take a toll on your well-being. If you find yourself feeling out of control, step back and ask yourself, "What exactly is causing me to feel this way?" For instance, does your boss contact you at all hours of the day and night, and make you feel as if you need to always be on call? Are the priorities within your workplace constantly shifting so you can never get ahead? Or do you simply not have enough predictability in terms of your physical or people resources to effectively perform your job?

Then ask yourself what you can do to shift this situation. Is it possible to discuss the issue with your boss to establish better boundaries and not respond to messages 24/7? Could you come to an agreement that certain priorities will remain constant? Or could you have more resources if you communicated about what you needed? Once you've considered these areas, you can then see what you can do to influence your environment versus what won't change no matter what you say or do.

3. Reward

If the extrinsic and intrinsic rewards for your job don't match the amount of effort and time you put into them, then you're likely to feel like the investment is not worth the payoff.

In these instances, you want to look within and determine exactly what you would need to feel properly appreciated. For example, perhaps you need to ask for a raise or promotion. Maybe you need more positive feedback and face time with your boss. Or perhaps you need to take advantage of the rewards you've already accrued, such as taking the comp time that you earned during a particularly busy time at the office. Experiment to see which rewards would make what you're doing worth it to you and whether there is the opportunity to receive more of those rewards within your current work environment.

4. Community

Who do you work with or around? How supportive and trusting are those relationships? In many cases you can't choose your colleagues and clients, but you can improve the dynamic. It could be as simple as taking the time to ask others how their day is going—and really listening. Or sending an email to someone to let them know you appreciated their presentation. Or choosing to communicate something difficult in a respectful, nonjudgmental way. Burnout can be contagious, so to elevate your individual engagement, you must shift the morale of the group. If you've found that once you've done all you can, others can't improve or don't want improved relationships, then you may want to consider a job change.

5. Fairness

Think about whether you believe that you receive fair and equitable treatment. For example, are you acknowledged for your contributions or are other individuals praised and your work goes unnoticed? Does someone else get regular deadline extensions or access to additional resources when you don't?

If you feel that a lack of fairness exacerbates your burnout, start by speaking up. Sometimes individuals are unaware of their biases or won't take action until you ask for what you want. You can request to be mentioned as a contributor, to give part of a presentation, or to have additional time and resources. And if you still find that the response seems inequitable, you can consider bringing that up in a polite way: "I noticed that the Chicago team got an additional week to work on their project that was originally due on the same date as ours. Can you help me understand why that's not possible for our team as well?"

6. Values Mismatch

If you highly value something that your company does not, your motivation to work hard and persevere can significantly drop. Ideals and motivations tend to be deeply ingrained in individuals and organizations. When you're assessing this element of burnout, you need to think carefully about how important it is to you to match your values with those of the organization.

Also consider whether the leaders in your company have shifted their values. Look around and ask yourself: How does my boss, my team, and my organization make decisions and invest resources? Do I feel good about those underlying motivations? Do they seem open to change? If you have strongly held values and those with influence in your organization differ from yours, you may need to look for a more congruent opportunity.

Burnout isn't simply about being tired. It's a multifaceted issue that requires a multifaceted solution.

Before you quit, really think through what *exactly* is contributing to your burnout and attempt to make changes. If you find that despite your best efforts, little has changed, then see if it makes sense to stay or if it's time to leave.

———————

Elizabeth Grace Saunders is a time management coach and the founder of Real Life E Time Coaching & Speaking. She is author of *How to Invest Your Time Like Money* and *Divine Time Management*. Find out more at www.RealLifeE.com.

CHAPTER 3

How to Get Through an Extremely Busy Time at Work

by Alice Boyes

You're an accountant deep in tax season, a junior doctor in residency, or an entrepreneur juggling a startup and a baby. Many of us go through seasons of life when we have very little personal time. Others may be committed to jobs that regularly involve intense and long hours, creating a long-term lack of rest.

Adapted from content posted on hbr.org, March 26, 2019 (product #H04V4S).

While this kind of overwork is not ideal, there are un-doubtedly situations in which it becomes a necessity or makes personal sense. I've certainly done it for periods of my life, for instance, in the lead-up to exams or to put fi-nal polishes on my books. At times like this, when having a full weekend off seems like a distant dream, advice on the importance of maintaining work-life balance, reduc-ing stress, and getting enough sleep can feel like a slap in the face. You don't need to be scolded to work less. You need practical tips for surviving and thriving when you have to be fully committed. Here are some strategies that can help.

Use Premack's Principle

Premack's principle (as it applies here) is to use an easier behavior as a reward for a harder behavior. For instance, you can reward yourself for finishing a cognitively de-manding task (like writing a complex report) by com-pleting a low-key but necessary task, like running an er-rand that helps you stay organized. This approach can help you pace yourself during your workday, ensuring that you get regular breaks during which your mind can shift into a more relaxed gear, while still being produc-tive. Think of it like recovering from bursts of running by walking instead of stopping.

Compartmentalize

Tasks you actually enjoy can become tense, unpleasant experiences if, while you're doing them, you're mentally elsewhere, feeling stressed and anxious about the other hundred things on your list. What's quite pleasurable or satisfying for you, even though it's time consuming? Perhaps it's figuring out how best to present an intricate data visualization. Maybe it's rehearsing speeches in front of friends or family.

If you know the task is important and you're approaching it efficiently, allow yourself to enjoy it. For recurrent hard assignments, think about the parts of it you like best at the beginning, middle, and end stages. For instance, I like listening to my Mac auto-read-aloud drafts of my blog posts when doing my final edits. It's satisfying to find those last few instances where I've repeated a word or made a typo, or the melody of a sentence is wrong. I also like the beginning stages of projects in which I get to top up my brain with broad searches on Google Scholar, and the middle stages when I'm wrestling with parts of what I'm writing that aren't working but when my overall structure is in place and sound. By articulating distinct, enjoyable aspects of tasks, you can be more mindful and savor them.

Save Small Scraps of Time for Mental Rest

When you're very busy, it's tempting to try to cram productive activity, like responding to email or thinking through decisions, into any small crack of time. This could be when you're standing in line at the supermarket, waiting for a presentation to start, or in the five minutes between finishing one thing and joining a meeting. When you're slammed, it can seem essential to work during these moments. However, you don't have to. Instead, consider using brief waiting times for true mental breaks. Take some slow breaths, drop your shoulders, and just chill.

You don't need to take an all-or-nothing approach to this tip, of course. If using small scraps of time to keep work moving sometimes suits you, keep doing it Monday to Friday, but on the weekend, consider giving yourself those little breaks. Find the balance that works for you.

Add Physical Decompression Rituals to Your Day

When we're overloaded, we can hold a lot of physical tension. This is partly due to our in-built fight/flight/freeze response to fear or stress. For instance, the evolutionary basis of balled fists is your cave-person self-preparing to run or punch. Some people breathe faster when they're stressed. Some adopt an aggressive, dominant tone of voice or body language. Since these reactions are often unconscious, you'll need prompts to correct them.

Try using context triggers—deciding which moments in the day you'll use to physically decompress. For instance, maybe you can take some slow breaths whenever you go to the bathroom, or just after you wake up or just before you get into bed. You can also use emotions as triggers like "When I notice I feel stressed, I'll scan my body for tension and soften and release any spots I find." If you're not sure how to do this, just try opening and closing your fists a few times, clenching and unclenching your jaw, or scrunching and dropping your shoulders. Our thoughts, emotions, and bodily reactions are a feedback loop. When you mimic the physiology of someone who is relaxed, you'll find that your thinking becomes less closed, and psychologically challenging activities in which you need to think openly, like taking in feedback, will seem easier.

Pair Pleasure Experiences with Other Activities

In my book *The Healthy Mind Toolkit*, I wrote about how people often put off pleasure, especially when they feel too busy or undeserving because they haven't gotten enough done. You can buffer yourself against the stress of feeling rushed and overloaded if you recurrently pair simple sources of pleasure with particular activities you're not as excited to do. For instance, I pack peanut butter sandwiches whenever I fly, which is about the only time I ever eat them, and now the two experiences are mentally linked. No matter how stressed I am about my trip or all the work I need to do before, during, and after it, I feel just a little bit more relaxed because I've packed that treat for myself. Or, if you love podcasts, perhaps you have a routine of listening to specific shows on your commute home each day of the week. If what you love isn't as simple as sandwiches or podcasts, set aside just a bit of consistent time to indulge in your interest, so you've removed decision making as a barrier. For instance, if cooking is your passion, perhaps you whip up a big batch of something on Sundays that you can then take as lunch for the week.

Just to be clear: I'm not saying that you can life-hack your way through being a permanent workaholic. But, during those times when, on balance, overworking makes short- or long-term sense (or is a necessity), you need some harm-minimization strategies. It's important to pace yourself and not let your obligations consume you.

———————

Alice Boyes, PhD, is a former clinical psychologist turned writer and is author of *The Healthy Mind Toolkit* and *The Anxiety Toolkit.*

CHAPTER 4

How to Avoid Burnout While Working from Home

by Laura M. Giurge and Vanessa K. Bohns

Millions around the globe made a sudden transition to remote work during the Covid-19 pandemic. At first, many employers were concerned about maintaining employee productivity. Later, some became concerned that this unprecedented situation carried a longer-term risk: employee burnout.

Adapted from "3 Tips to Avoid WFH Burnout," on hbr.org, April 3, 2020 (product #H05IX0).

The risk of burnout when working from home is substantial. The lines between work and nonwork tend to blur. Employees who are working remotely for the first time are especially likely to struggle to preserve healthy boundaries between their professional and personal lives.

Lots of research suggests that drawing lines between our professional and personal lives is crucial, especially for our mental health. But it's difficult, even in the best of circumstances. In no small measure, that's because the knowledge economy has radically transformed what it means to be an "ideal worker."

Our research has shown that workers often unintentionally make it hard for their supervisors, colleagues, and employees to maintain boundaries. One way they do so is by sending work emails outside office hours. In five studies involving more than 2,000 working adults, we found that senders of after-hours work emails underestimate how compelled receivers feel to respond right away, even when such emails are not urgent.

Covid-19 amplified these pressures. Even for employees who have a natural preference to separate their work and personal lives, circumstances might not allow them to do so. When schools and daycares closed, additional burdens were placed on working parents or low-income workers. Even companies that already encouraged employees to work from home were likely to have some trouble when supporting employees who faced the many challenges of working at home in the presence of their families.

So how can you continue to compartmentalize your work life and nonwork life? How can you "leave your work at the door" if you are no longer going out the door? And what can employers, managers, and coworkers do to help one another cope?

Based on our research and the wider academic literature, here are some recommendations.

Maintain Physical and Social Boundaries

In a classic paper, Blake Ashforth of Arizona State University described the ways in which people demarcate the transition from work to nonwork roles via "boundary-crossing activities."[1] Putting on your work clothes, commuting from home to work—these are physical and social indicators that something has changed. You've transitioned from "home you" to "work you."

Try to maintain these boundaries when working remotely. In the short term, it may be a welcome change not to have to catch an early train to work, or to be able to spend all day in your pajamas—but both of those things are boundary-crossing activities that can do you good, so don't abandon them altogether. Put on your work clothes every morning—casual Friday is fine, of course, but get yourself ready nonetheless. And consider replacing your morning commute with a walk to a nearby park, or even just around your apartment, before sitting down to work.

Maintain Temporal Boundaries as Much as Possible

Maintaining temporal boundaries is critical for well-being and work engagement. This is particularly true when so many employees—and/or their colleagues—are facing the challenge of integrating childcare or elder-care responsibilities during regular work hours. It's challenging even for employees without children or other family responsibilities, thanks to the mobile devices that keep our work with us at all times.

Sticking to a 9-to-5 schedule may prove unrealistic. You need to find work-time budgets that function best for yourself. You also need to be conscious and respectful that others might work at different times than you do. For some, it might be during a child's nap; for others, it might be when their partner is cooking dinner. Whether or not you have children, you can create intentional work-time budgets by adding an "out of office" reply during certain hours of the day to focus on work. A less-extreme reply might just let others know that you might be slower than usual in responding, decreasing response expectations for others and yourself. If your flexible schedule requires you to work early or late, you can also add a note in your email footer indicating that while you might send messages outside regular office hours, you have no expectation of receiving a response outside their regular office hours.

Creating clear temporal boundaries often depends on your ability to coordinate your time with others. This calls for leaders to aid employees in structuring, coordinating, and managing the pace of work. This might mean regularly holding virtual check-in meetings with employees or providing them with tools to create virtual coffee breaks or workspaces.

Focus on Your Most Important Work

While working from home, you may feel compelled to project the appearance of productivity, but this can lead you to work on tasks that are more immediate instead of more important—a tendency that research suggests is counterproductive in the long run, even if it benefits productivity in the short run. Particularly if you are facing an increased workload as you are juggling family and work tasks, you should pay attention to prioritizing important work.

Working all the time, even on your most important tasks, isn't the answer. According to some estimates, a knowledge worker is only productive three hours every day, on average, and these hours should be free of interruptions or multitasking. Even before Covid-19, employees found it difficult to carve out three continuous hours to focus on their core work tasks. When work and family boundaries are removed, employees' time is even more fragmented.

If you feel "on" all the time, you are at a higher risk of burnout when working from home than if you were going to the office as usual. In the long term, trying to squeeze in work and email responses whenever you have a few minutes to do so—during nap time, on the weekend, or by pausing a movie in the evening—is not only counterproductive but also detrimental to your well-being. We all need to find new ways—and help others do the same—to carve out nonwork time and mental space.

These are just a few recommendations that can help you maintain boundaries between your work and your personal life and thereby avoid burnout in the long run. Use the flexibility that remote work affords you to experiment with how to make your circumstances work for you.

———————

Laura M. Giurge is a postdoctoral research associate at London Business School and the Barnes Research Fellow at the Wellbeing Research Centre at the University of Oxford. Her research focuses on time, happiness, and the future of work. **Vanessa K. Bohns** is an associate professor of organizational behavior at the ILR School at Cornell University.

NOTE

1. Blake E. Ashforth, Mel Fugate, and Glen E. Kreiner, "All in a Day's Work: Boundaries and Micro Role Transitions," *Academy of Management Review*, July 2000.

CHAPTER 5

Making Compassion a Habit

by Annie McKee and Kandi Wiens

"I am sick to death of the ridiculous situations I have to deal with at work. The pettiness, the politics, the stupidity—it's out of control. This kind of thing stresses me out to the max."

Stress is a happiness killer. And life is just too short to be unhappy at work. But we hear this kind of thing all the time from leaders in industries as varied as financial services, education, pharmaceuticals, and health care. In our coaching and consulting, we're seeing a spike

---

Adapted from "Prevent Burnout by Making Compassion a Habit," on hbr.org, May 11, 2017 (product #H03NLJ).

in the number of leaders who used to love their jobs but now say things like "I'm not sure it's worth it anymore." They're burned out—emotionally exhausted and cynical—as a result of chronic and acute work stress.

Why is stress on the rise? A lot of it has to do with uncertainty in the world and constant changes in our organizations. Many people are overworking, putting in more hours than ever before. The lines between work and home have blurred or disappeared. Add to that persistent (sometimes even toxic) conflicts with bosses and coworkers that put us on guard and make us irritable. Under these circumstances, our performance and well-being suffer. Work feels like a burden. Burnout is just around the corner. And happiness at work is not even a remote possibility.

Here's the good news: Some people *don't* get burned out. They continue to thrive despite the difficult conditions in their workplace.

Why? The answer lies in part with empathy, an emotional intelligence competency packed with potent stress-taming powers. Empathy is "compassion in action." When you engage empathy, you seek to understand people's needs, desires, and point of view. You feel and express genuine concern for their well-being, and then *you act on it*.

One of our studies (Kandi's research on executive-level health-care leaders) confirms this.[1] When asked how they deal with chronic and acute work stress, 91% of the study's executives described how expressing empathy allows them to stop focusing on themselves and connect with others on a much deeper level. Other research-ers agree: Expressing empathy produces physiological effects that calm us in the moment and strengthen our long-term sustainability.[2] It evokes responses in our bodies that arouse the (good) parasympathetic nervous system, and it reverses the effects of the stress response brought on by the (bad) sympathetic nervous system. So not only do others benefit from our empathy, but we benefit, too.

Based on our research, Annie's with leaders in global companies and Kandi's with health-care leaders, we of-fer a two-part strategy that can help unleash empathy and break the burnout cycle. First, you need to practice self-compassion. Then you will be ready to change some of your habitual ways of dealing with people so you—and they—can benefit from your empathy.

Practice Self-Compassion

If you really want to deal with stress, you've got to stop trying to be a hero and start caring for and about yourself. Self-compassion involves: (1) seeking to truly *understand* yourself and what you are experiencing emo-tionally, physically, and intellectually at work; (2) *caring* for yourself, as opposed to shutting down; and (3) *acting* to help yourself. Here are two practical ways to practice self-compassion:

- **Curb the urge to overwork.** When the pressure is on at work, we're often tempted to work more hours to "get on top of things." But overwork is a trap, not a solution. Just doing more—and more, and more, and more—rarely fixes problems, and it usually makes things worse, because we are essentially manufacturing our own stress. We shut the proverbial door on people and problems, thinking that if we can get away, we can at least do our job without getting caught up in others' drama. When nothing changes or it gets worse, we give up. This is a vicious cycle: Overwork leads to more stress, which leads to isolation, which causes us to give up, which leads to even more stress. So, instead of putting in more hours when you're stressed, find ways to renew yourself. Exercise, practice mindfulness, spend more time with loved ones, and dare we say, get more sleep.

- **Stop beating yourself up.** Stress is often the result of being too hard on ourselves when we fail or don't meet our own expectations. We forget to treat ourselves as living, breathing, feeling human beings. Instead of letting self-criticism stress you out, acknowledge how you feel, acknowledge that others would feel similarly in the same situation, and be kind and forgiving to yourself. Shifting your mindset from *threatened* to *self-compassion* will strengthen your resiliency.

Give Empathy

Taking steps toward self-compassion will prepare you emotionally to reach out to others. But let's face it, empathy is not the norm in many workplaces. In fact, lack of empathy and even depersonalization of others are symptoms of the emotional exhaustion that comes with burnout. Here are a few tips to make empathy part of your normal way of dealing with people at work.

- **Build friendships with people you like at work.** Most people can rattle off a dozen reasons why you shouldn't be friends with people at work. We believe just the opposite. Real connections and friendships at work matter—a lot. According to the Harvard Grant Study, one of the longest-running longitudinal studies of human development, having warm relationships is essential to health, well-being, and happiness.[3] Other research shows that caring for and feeling cared for by others lowers our blood pressure, enhances our immunity, and leads to overall better health.

- **Value people for who they really are.** The "ridiculous situations" mentioned by the leader at the beginning of this article are often the result of miscommunication and misunderstanding. Instead of really listening, we hear what we want to, which is misinformed by biases and stereotypes. It gets in the way of our ability to understand and connect with others. The resulting conflicts cause a lot of unnecessary stress. To prevent this, be curious about people. Ask yourself, "How can I understand where this person is coming from?" Listen with an open mind so that you gain their trust, which is good for your stress level and your ability to influence them.

- **Coach people.** According to research by Richard Boyatzis, Melvin Smith, and 'Alim Beveridge, coaching others has positive psychophysiological effects that restore the body's natural healing and growth processes and improves stamina.[4] When we care enough to invest time in developing others, we become less preoccupied with ourselves, which balances the toxic effects of stress and burnout.

- **Put your customers, clients, or patients at the center of your conversations.** If misaligned goals with coworkers are a source of your stress, try physically moving your conversations to a place where you can put other people's needs at the center. One chief medical officer who participated in Kandi's study described a time when he had an intense, stressful argument with two other physicians about the treatment plan for a terminally ill cancer patient. They were in a conference room debating and debating, with no progress on a decision. Seeing that everyone's professional conduct was declining and stress levels were rising, the CMO decided to take the conversation to the patient's room. He sat on one side of the patient's bed, holding her hand. The other two physicians sat on the opposite side of the bed, holding her other hand. They began talking again, but this time *literally* with the patient at the center of their conversation. As the CMO said, "The conversation took on a very different tone when we were able to refocus. Everyone was calm. It brought us to the same level. We were connected. It was a very effective antidote to stress."

One caution about empathy and compassion: They can be powerful forces in our fight against stress—until they aren't. Caring too much can hurt. Overextending your empathy can take a toll on your emotional resources and lead to compassion fatigue, a phenomenon that occurs when compassion becomes a burden and results in even more stress. (See the sidebar "When Empathy Is Exhausting" at the end of this chapter.) So pay close attention to your limits and develop strategies to rein in excessive empathy if it gets out of control.

It's worth the risk, though. Once you commit to caring about yourself, you can start to care about others, and in the process you will create resonant relationships that are both good for you and good for the people you work with.

———————

Annie McKee is a senior fellow at the University of Pennsylvania Graduate School of Education and the director of the PennCLO Executive Doctoral Program. She is the author of *How to Be Happy at Work* and a coauthor of *Primal Leadership, Resonant Leadership*, and *Becoming a Resonant Leader*. **Kandi Wiens, EdD,** is a senior fellow at the University of Pennsylvania Graduate School of Education in the PennCLO Executive Doctoral Program and director of the Penn Master's in Medical Education Program. She is also an executive coach, national speaker, and organizational change consultant.

WHEN EMPATHY IS EXHAUSTING

by Adam Waytz

Though empathy is essential to leading and managing others—without it, you'll make disastrous decisions—failing to recognize its limits can impair individual and organizational performance.

Like heavy-duty cognitive tasks, such as keeping multiple pieces of information in mind at once or avoiding distractions in a busy environment, empathy depletes our mental resources. So jobs that require constant empathy can lead to "compassion fatigue," an acute inability to empathize that's driven by stress, and burnout, a more gradual and chronic version of this phenomenon.

Health and human services professionals (doctors, nurses, social workers, corrections officers) are especially at risk, because empathy is central to their day-to-day jobs. In a study of hospice nurses, for example, the key predictors for compassion fatigue were psychological: anxiety, feelings of trauma, life demands, and what the researchers call excessive empathy, meaning the tendency to sacrifice one's own needs for others' (rather than simply "feeling" for people). Variables such as long hours and heavy caseloads also had an impact, but less than expected. And in a survey of Korean nurses, self-reported compassion fatigue strongly predicted their intentions to leave their jobs in the near future. Other studies of nurses show additional consequences of compassion fatigue, such as absenteeism and increased errors in administering medication.

People who work for charities and other nonprofits (think animal shelters) are similarly at risk. Voluntary turnover is exceedingly high, in part because of the empathically demanding nature of the work; low pay exacerbates the element of self-sacrifice. What's more, society's strict views of how nonprofits should operate mean they face a backlash when they act like businesses (for instance, investing in "overhead" to keep the organization running smoothly). They're expected to thrive through selfless outpourings of compassion from workers.

The demand for empathy is relentless in other sectors as well. Day after day, managers must motivate knowledge workers by understanding their experiences and perspectives and helping them find personal meaning in their work. Customer service professionals must continually quell the concerns of distressed callers. Empathy is exhausting in any setting or role in which it's a primary aspect of the job.

Adam Waytz is a psychologist and associate professor of management and organizations at the Kellogg School of Management at Northwestern University.

Adapted from "The Limits of Empathy," in *Harvard Business Review*, January 2016 (product #R1601D).

NOTES

1. Kandi Wiens, "Leading Through Burnout: The Influence of Emotional Intelligence on the Ability of Executive Level Physician Leaders to Cope with Occupational Stress and Burnout" (diss., University of Pennsylvania, 2016).

2. Kathryn Birnie, Michael Speca, and Linda E. Carlson, "Exploring Self-compassion and empathy in the Context of Mindfulness-based Stress Reduction (MBSR)," Stress and Health, 2010, https://self-compassion.org/wp-content/uploads/publications/MBSR-Exploring_self-compassion_empathy_in_the_context_of_mindfulness_based_stress_reduction.pdf; Helen Riess, "The Power of Empathy," TEDxMiddlebury, December 12, 2013, https://www.youtube.com/watch?v=baHrcC8B4WM; Richard J. Davidson, "Toward a Biology of Positive Affect and Compassion," *Visions of Compassion: Western Scientists and Tibetan Buddhists Examine Human Nature*, eds. Richard J. Davidson and Anne Harrington (New York: Oxford University Press, 2002).

3. Robert Waldinger, "What Makes a Good Life? Lessons from the Longest Study on Happiness," TEDxBeaconStreet, November 2015, https://www.ted.com/talks/robert_waldinger_what_makes_a_good_life_lessons_from_the_longest_study_on_happiness?language=en.

4. Richard Boyatzis, Melvin Smith, and 'Alim Beveridge, "Coaching with Compassion: Inspiring Health, Well-Being, and Development in Organizations," *Journal of Applied Behavioral Science* 49, no. 2 (2013).

CHAPTER 6

Collaboration Without Burnout

by Rob Cross, Scott Taylor, and Deb Zehner

"So many different people can get to you through different channels, and the pressure is enormous."

"Constant email, international travel, calls at all hours—I was exhausted. The collaborative demands eventually wore me down."

"I always felt I had to do more, go further, save the day. I would become people's life raft and then almost drown."

These are the voices of collaborative overload.

As organizations become more global, adopt matrixed structures, offer increasingly complex products and services, and enable 24/7 communication, they are

Adapted from an article in *Harvard Business Review*, July 2018 (product #R1804L).

requiring employees to collaborate with more internal colleagues and external contacts than ever before. According to research from Connected Commons, most managers now spend 85% or more of their work time on email, in meetings, and on the phone, and the demand for such activities has jumped by 50% over the past decade. Companies benefit, of course: Faster innovation and more-seamless client service are two by-products of greater collaboration. But along with all this comes significantly less time for focused individual work, careful reflection, and sound decision making. A 2016 HBR article coauthored by one of us dubbed this destructive phenomenon *collaborative overload* and suggested ways that organizations might combat it.

Over the past few years we've conducted further research—both quantitative and qualitative—to better understand the problem and uncover solutions that individuals can implement on their own. Working with 20 global organizations in diverse fields (software, consumer products, professional services, manufacturing, and life sciences), we started by creating models of employees' collaborations and considering the effect of those interactions on engagement, performance, and voluntary attrition. We then used network analyses to identify efficient collaborators—people who work productively with a wide variety of others but use the least amount of their own and their colleagues' time—and interviewed 200 of them (100 men and 100 women) about their working lives. We learned a great deal about how overload happens and what leaders must do to avoid it so that they can continue to thrive.

Not surprisingly, we found that always-on work cultures, encroaching technology, demanding bosses, difficult clients, and inefficient coworkers were a big part of the problem, and most of those challenges do require organizational solutions. But we discovered in many cases that external time sinks were matched by another enemy: individuals' own mindsets and habits. Fortunately, people can overcome those obstacles themselves, right away, with some strategic self-management.

We uncovered best practices in three broad categories: *beliefs* (understanding why we take on too much); *role, schedule, and network* (eliminating unnecessary collaboration to make time for work that is aligned with professional aspirations and personal values); and *behavior* (ensuring that necessary or desired collaborative work is as productive as possible). Not all our recommendations will suit everyone: People's needs differ by personality, hierarchical level, and work context. But we found that when the people we studied took action on just four or five of them, they were able to claw back 18% to 24% of their collaborative time.

Two Types of Overload

Collaborative overload generally occurs in either a surge or a slow burn. A surge can result from a promotion, a request from a boss or a colleague to take on or help out with a project, or the desire to jump into an "extracurricular" work activity because you feel obligated or don't want to miss out. Consider Mike, an insurance company executive who was already managing multiple projects— one of which had his entire team working day and night to turn around a struggling segment of the business. When his boss asked him to help create a new unit that would allow the company to present a single face to the market, he felt he couldn't say no. It was a great development opportunity—to which his skills were perfectly suited—and it offered prime exposure to senior management. Yet he couldn't abandon his existing team in the midst of its work. So he decided to do both jobs at once.

A slow burn is more insidious and occurs through incremental increases in the volume, diversity, and pace of collaborative demands over time, as personal effectiveness leads to larger networks and greater scope of responsibilities. Go-to people in organizations suffer from this type of overload. As we gain experience, we often tend to take on more work, and our identities start to become intertwined with accomplishment, helping, or being in the know. We tend not to question what we are doing as we add tasks or work late into the night on email. And, of course, our colleagues welcome these tendencies; as we gain reputations for competence and responsiveness, people in our networks bring us more work and requests. Ellen, an 18-year veteran of a *Fortune* 100 technology company, is a case in point. She was fiercely driven and took pride in her ability to help colleagues, solve problems, and cut through bureaucracy to get things done. Eventually, however, she felt weighed down by a list of projects and commitments that were "beyond the realm of doable."

Though Mike's and Ellen's situations are different, our research suggests that the solutions to their and others' overload problems are similar. They cannot continue to work the same way they always have and remain effective. They need to take better charge of their working lives.

Why We Take on Too Much

The first step in combating collaborative overload is to recognize how much of it is driven by your own desire to maintain a reputation as a helpful, knowledgeable, or influential colleague or to avoid the anxiety that stems from ceding control over or declining to participate in group work. For example, someone who engages in the entire life cycle of a small project, beyond the time when the need for her expertise has passed, might pride herself on supporting teammates and ensuring a high-quality result. But that's not the kind of collaboration that makes a difference over the long term; indeed, too much of it will prevent her from doing more-important work.

Knowing why you accept collaborative work—above and beyond what your manager and your company demand—is how you begin to combat overload. When we counsel executives, we ask them to reflect on the specific identity-based triggers that most often lead them into overload. For example:

- Do you crave the feeling of accomplishment that comes from ticking less challenging items off your to-do list?

- Does your ambition to be influential or recognized for your expertise cause you to attend meetings or discussions that don't truly require your involvement?

- Do you pride yourself on being always ready to answer questions and pitch in on group work?

- Do you agree to take on collaborative activities because you're worried about being labeled a poor performer or not a team player?

- Are you uncomfortable staying away from certain issues or projects because you fear missing out on something or aren't sure the work will be done right without you?

Most executives we've encountered answer yes to one if not several of those questions.

Efficient collaborators remember that saying yes to something always means saying no to—or participating less fully in—something else. They remind themselves that small wins (an empty inbox, a perfectly worded report, a single client call) are not always important ones. They think carefully about their areas of expertise and determine when they do, or don't, have value to add. They stop seeing themselves as indispensable and shift the source of their self-worth so that it comes from not just showcasing their own capabilities but also stepping away to let others develop theirs and gain visibility.

As one executive told us, "I have come to the realization that if people really need me, they will find me. I am probably skipping 30% of my meetings now, and work seems to be getting done just fine."

When Mike found himself at a breaking point with his twin projects, he realized how much of his self-worth derived from always saying yes to—and then achieving—

the goals suggested to him. "It took falling down and a patient spouse to really see this pattern," he says. He decided that he needed to set clear priorities in both his career and his personal life. "Then saying no was not about my not coming through but about maintaining focus on what mattered."

Ellen, too, realized that her self-image as a helper—constantly looking for opportunities to contribute and never declining a request—had become problematic. "The difficult part is recognizing this tendency in the moment and working hard not to jump in," she acknowledges. "But I told my team how important this was and also asked a few people to be 'truth tellers' who caution me when they see it happening."

Eliminating the Unnecessary

Next you'll need to restructure your role, schedule, and network to avoid the triggers you've identified and reduce or eliminate unnecessary collaboration. Rather than thinking things will get better on their own, living reactively, and falling into patterns dictated by other people's objectives, efficient collaborators play offense on collaborative overload. They clarify their "north star" objectives—the strengths they want to employ in their work and the values they want to embody, in the context of their organization's priorities—and then streamline their working lives in a way that buffers them against nonaligned requests.

Start by reviewing your calendar and email communications on a regular basis, using a tool such as Microsoft's MyAnalytics or Cisco's "human network intelligence" platform. Look back four or five months to identify recurring group activities, meetings, or exchanges that aren't core to your success and could be declined or offered to others as a developmental opportunity. Consider decisions you're being pulled into unnecessarily and how processes or teams might be changed so that you needn't be involved. Recognize when you're being sought out for information or expertise in areas no longer central to your role or ambitions and figure out whether you could share your knowledge more widely on your company's intranet or if another go-to person might derive greater benefit from that collaboration.

At the same time, work to reset colleagues' expectations about the level and timeliness of your engagement. Clarify, for example, that not responding to a group email or opting out of a meeting does not mean you lack interest or appreciation. Talk about your key priorities so that everyone knows what you need (and want) to spend the most time on. Ask colleagues about their interests and ambitions so that you can identify opportunities to distribute or delegate work. A key inflection point for all the executives we've counseled has been when they start seeing requests for collaboration as ways to activate and engage those in their networks rather than as adding to their own to-do lists.

Finally, block out time for reflective work and seek collaboration with those who can help you move toward your north star objectives. Mike focused on building capabilities in the business unit he directed. Instead of jumping at unrelated projects for political exposure, he began to differentiate himself through expertise and his team's contribution. Ellen's strategy was to create exceptionally clear boundaries: "I am there 8 a.m. to 6 p.m., and people know I give 100% then. But after that I don't let myself get drawn into unnecessary email, calls, or late-night work just to help out."

Another leader described the shift like this: "Playing defense sucks. You are always reactive and living in fear. The only way to escape it is to get clarity on who you are and what you want to do and start forging a path and network that enable you to get there."

Keeping It Productive

Once you've taken stock of your collaborative workload, it's time to enhance the value of the collaboration you've chosen to participate in. Our research suggests that poorly run meetings are the biggest time sink in organizations. Even if you don't control the ones you attend, you can make them more productive by, for example, asking the leader to circulate an agenda or a pre-read before the gathering and a short email on agreements, commitments, and next steps afterward. You can also limit your involvement by explaining that you have a hard stop (real or constructed) so that you're not stuck when others run overtime, and asking to attend only those portions for which you are needed or agreeing to half the time a colleague or employee requests. It's crucial to establish norms early on in any relationship or group. If you wait, problems will become harder to address.

You can also institute or encourage new norms for emails by addressing format (for example, observing a maximum length and choosing an outline structure with bullets, as opposed to full-text paragraphs), the use of "cc" and "reply all," and appropriate response times for various types of requests. Consider virtual collaboration tools (such as Google Docs), which offer a better medium for work that is exploratory (defining a problem space or brainstorming solutions) or integrative (when people with varying expertise, perspectives, or work assignments need to produce a joint solution). The key is to ensure that you're using the right tools at the right time and not worsening collaborative demands. You should also learn to recognize when a conversation has become too complicated or contentious for email or chat and switch to a more efficient phone call or face-to-face meeting.

For one-on-one interactions, always consider whether you are consuming your counterpart's time efficiently. Ask yourself, "Am I clear on what I want to accomplish from a meeting or a conversation?" And invite others to be equally disciplined by asking early on, "So that I use your time well, would you quickly let me know what you hope we can accomplish together?"

When it comes to building your network, focus on the quality of the relationships, not the number of connections. We repeatedly found that efficient collaborators draw people to collaborative work by conferring status, envisioning joint success, diffusing ownership, and generating a sense of purpose and energy around an outcome. By creating "pull"—rather than simply pushing their agenda—they get greater and more-aligned participation and build trust so that people don't feel the need to seek excessive input or approval.

Ellen, for example, decided to engage stakeholders in collaborative work early to save time later in the process. "I used to dot every i and cross every t before approaching others," she says. "But I've learned that if I get a plan partially developed and then bring in my team, my boss, even my clients, they get invested and help me spot flaws, and I avoid tons of downstream work to fix things or convince people." Another leader we know schedules one-on-ones with direct reports to discuss priorities, values, and personal aspirations, enhancing their ability to work together efficiently as a team in the future. "There are so many ways people can misinterpret actions and then cause a lot of churn later," he says. "If I spend the time to give them a sense of where I'm coming from, it saves all sorts of time in unnecessary collaborations."

Conclusion

The recent explosion in the volume and diversity of collaborative demands is a reality that's here to stay. Unfortunately, the invisible nature of these demands means that few organizations are managing collaborative activity strategically. So it falls to you, the individual, to fight overload and reclaim your collaborative time.

Rob Cross is the Edward A. Madden Professor of Global Leadership at Babson College and a coauthor of *The Hidden Power of Social Networks* (Harvard Business Review

Press, 2004). **Scott Taylor** is an associate professor of organizational behavior at Babson College. **Deb Zehner** has 15 years of experience conducting research, developing network-based assets, and leading organizational network projects, most recently with Connected Commons.

Bouncing Back from Burnout

CHAPTER 7

Beating Burnout

by Monique Valcour

Heavy workloads and deadline pressures are a fact of managerial life. Who doesn't feel overwhelmed or stretched thin sometimes? But when relentless work stress pushes you into the debilitating state we call burnout, it is a serious problem, affecting not just your own performance and well-being, both on the job and off, but also that of your team and your organization.

Hard data on the prevalence of burnout is elusive. Some researchers say that as few as 7% of professionals have been seriously impacted by burnout. But others have documented rates as high as 50% among medical residents and 85% among financial professionals. Research has also linked burnout to many negative physical

---

Adapted from an article in *Harvard Business Review*, November 2016 (product #R1611H).

and mental health outcomes, including coronary artery disease, hypertension, sleep disturbances, depression, and anxiety, as well as to increased alcohol and drug use. Moreover, burnout has been shown to produce feelings of futility and alienation, undermine the quality of relationships, and diminish long-term career prospects.

Consider the case of Barbara (last name withheld), the CEO of a PR firm that serves technology industry clients. During the 2001 collapse of the dot-com bubble, the challenge of keeping her business afloat added extra stress to an already intense workload. Focused on this "unrelenting hustle," she neglected her health, lost perspective, and began to doubt her own abilities. Cheryl (not her real name), a partner in the Philadelphia office of a global law firm, hit the same sort of wall after she agreed to take on multiple leadership roles there in addition to managing her full-time legal practice. "I felt like my body was running on adrenaline—trying to do a marathon at a sprint pace—all the time," she recalls. And yet she couldn't step back mentally from work. Another executive I know—let's call him Ari—felt trapped in his role as a consultant at a boutique firm. Toxic internal dynamics and client relationship practices that clashed with his values had eroded his sense of self to the point where he didn't know how to go on—or get out.

Over the past 15 years as a coach, researcher, and educator, I've helped thousands of clients, students, and executive-development program participants in similar predicaments learn to manage the stress that can cause burnout and to ultimately achieve more-sustainable career success. The process involves noticing and acknowledging the symptoms, examining the underlying causes, and developing preventive strategies to counteract your particular pattern of burnout.

Three Components

Thanks to the pioneering research of psychologist Christina Maslach and several collaborators, we know that burnout is a three-component syndrome that arises in response to chronic stressors on the job. Let's examine each symptom—exhaustion, cynicism, and inefficacy—in turn.

Exhaustion is the central symptom of burnout. It comprises profound physical, cognitive, and emotional fatigue that undermines people's ability to work effectively and feel positive about what they're doing. This can stem from the demands of an always-on, 24/7 organizational culture, intense time pressure, or simply having too much to do, especially when you lack control over your work, dislike it, or don't have the necessary skills to accomplish it. In a state of exhaustion, you find that you're unable to concentrate or see the big picture; even routine and previously enjoyable tasks seem arduous, and it becomes difficult to drag yourself both into and out of the office. This is how burnout started for Cheryl. Her fuel tank was low, and it wasn't being adequately replenished.

Cynicism, also called depersonalization, represents an erosion of engagement. It is essentially a way of distancing yourself psychologically from your work. Instead of feeling invested in your assignments, projects, colleagues, customers, and other collaborators, you feel detached, negative, even callous. Cynicism can be the result of work overload, but it is also likely to occur in the presence of high conflict, unfairness, and lack of participation in decision making. For example, after ignoring repeated directives to push solutions that didn't solve clients' problems, Ari realized that the constant battle with his bosses was affecting his own behavior. "I was talking trash and shading the truth more often than I was being respectful and honest," he explains. Persistent cynicism is a signal that you have lost your connection to, enjoyment of, and pride in your work.

Inefficacy refers to feelings of incompetence and a lack of achievement and productivity. People with this symptom of burnout feel their skills slipping and worry that they won't be able to succeed in certain situations or accomplish certain tasks. It often develops in tandem with exhaustion and cynicism because people can't perform at their peak when they're out of fuel and have lost their connection to work. For example, although Barbara was a seasoned PR professional, the stress of the dot-com crisis and her resulting fatigue caused her to question her ability to serve clients and keep the business thriving. But burnout can also start with inefficacy if you lack the resources and support to do your job well, including adequate time, information, clear expectations, autonomy, and good relationships with those whose involvement you need to succeed. The absence of feedback and meaningful recognition, which leaves you wondering about the quality of your work and feeling that it's unappreciated, can also activate this component. This was the situation for Ari, who felt that he was forced to function at a subpar level because his organization didn't care enough to support good performance.

While each component is correlated with the other two and one often leads to another, individuals also have distinct burnout profiles. Michael Leiter, a longtime collaborator with Maslach, is examining this in his current research (see chapter 24 of this guide). He has found, for example, that some people are mainly exhausted but haven't yet developed cynicism or begun to doubt their performance. Others are primarily cynical or suffer most from feelings of reduced efficacy. People can also be high on two components and low on one. Although most of the prevention and recovery strategies we'll discuss are designed to address all three symptoms, it's a good idea to diagnose your specific burnout profile so that you know where you need the most help.

Recovery and Prevention

Situational factors are the biggest contributors to burnout, so changes at the job, team, or organizational level are often required to address all the underlying issues. However, there are steps you can take on your own once you're aware of the symptoms and of what might be causing them. Here are some strategies I have found to be successful with my clients.

Prioritize self-care

It's essential to replenish your physical and emotional energy, along with your capacity to focus, by prioritizing good sleep habits, nutrition, exercise, social connection, and practices that promote equanimity and well-being, like meditating, journaling, and enjoying nature. If you're having troubling squeezing such activities into your packed schedule, give yourself a week to assess exactly how you're spending your time. (You can do this on paper, in a spreadsheet, or on one of the many relevant apps now available.) For each block of time, record what you're doing, whom you're with, how you feel (for example, on a scale of 1 to 10, where 1 equals angry or drained and 10 is joyful or energized), and how valuable the activity is. This will help you find opportunities to limit your exposure to tasks, people, and situations that aren't essential and put you in a negative mood; increase your investment in those that boost your energy; and make space for restful, positive time away from work.

Barbara says she bounced back from her bout of burnout by "learning to do things that fill me up." Nowadays, when she notices that she's feeling overly tired or starting to doubt herself, she changes her behavior immediately, making use of flexible work options, hosting walking meetings to get out of the office, and setting limits on the amount of time she spends reading emails and taking calls from colleagues and clients.

After her crisis, Cheryl also became much more intentional about her time off. "I find that going away, getting a change of scenery, and 'taking it down a notch' allows my body and mind to rejuvenate," she says. "And my creativity benefits: I have more 'aha' moments, and I'm better able to connect the dots."

Shift your perspective

While rest, relaxation, and replenishment can ease exhaustion, curb cynicism, and enhance efficacy, they don't fully address the root causes of burnout. Back at the office, you may still face the same impossible work-load, untenable conflicts, or paltry resources. So now you must take a close look at your mindset and assumptions. What aspects of your situation are truly fixed, and which can you change? Altering your perspective can buffer the negative impact of even the inflexible aspects. If exhaustion is a key problem, ask yourself which tasks—including critical ones—you could delegate to free up meaningful time and energy for other important work. Are there ways to reshape your job in order to gain more control or to focus on the most fulfilling tasks? If cynicism is a major issue, can you shield yourself from the parts of the organization that frustrate you, while reengaging in your specific role and the whole enterprise? Or could you build some positive, supportive relationships to counteract the ones that drain you? And if you're feeling ineffective, what assistance or development might you seek out? If recognition is lacking, could you engage in some personal branding to showcase your work?

Cheryl worked with an executive coach to evaluate and reset her priorities. "I work in a competitive field and I'm a competitive person, which can skew the way you see reality," she explains. "In the past I didn't dare say no to leadership opportunities because I was afraid that if I did, everything might disappear." She says she's now replaced that "scarcity" mentality with one that instead presumes abundance. "Now if I feel overextended, I'll ask myself, Is there a way to inject joy back into this role, or is it time to give it up? And I understand that when I want to take something on, I need to decide what to give up to make space."

Ari did the same sort of deep thinking. Although he had previously felt tethered to his job—the firm was prestigious, the pay was good—he realized that values and ethics meant more to him than any perk, so he eventually quit and started his own business. "After I pushed back a couple of times and said that what we were recommending wasn't right for the clients, my boss cranked up the pressure on me and assigned me to only the most difficult clients. At one point I said to my wife, 'It might be good if I got hit by a bus. I don't want to die, but I'd like to be injured enough that I'd have to stop working for a while.' She said, 'That's it; you're getting out of there.'" He took a few months to line up some independent consulting assignments and then made the move.

Reduce exposure to job stressors

You'll also need to target high-value activities and relationships that still trigger unhealthy stress. This involves resetting the expectations of colleagues, clients, and even family members for what and how much you're willing to take on, as well as ground rules for working together. You may get pushback. But doubters must know that you're making these changes to improve your long-term productivity and protect your health.

Barbara, for example, is keenly aware of the aspects of PR work that put people in her field at risk of burnout, so now she actively manages them. "There's constant pressure, from both clients and the media," she explains. "But a lot of times, what clients label a crisis is not actually one. Part of the job is helping them put things in perspective. And being a good service professional doesn't mean you have to be a servant. You shouldn't be emailing at 11 at night on a regular basis."

Cheryl, too, says she's learned "not to get carried along in the current" of overwhelming demands. She adds, "You have to know when saying no is the right answer. And it takes courage and conviction to stick to your guns and not feel guilty." If you find that there are few or no opportunities to shift things in a more positive direction, you might want to contemplate a bigger change, as Ari did.

Seek out connections

The best antidote to burnout, particularly when it's driven by cynicism and inefficacy, is seeking out rich interpersonal interactions and continual personal and professional development. Find coaches and mentors who can help you identify and activate positive relationships and learning opportunities. Volunteering to advise others is another particularly effective way of breaking out of a negative cycle.

Given the influence of situational factors on burnout, it's likely that others in your organization are suffering too. If you band together to offer mutual support, identify problems, and brainstorm and advocate for solutions, you will all increase your sense of control and connection. Barbara participates in a CEO mentoring and advisory program called Vistage. "We're a small group of CEOs in noncompetitive businesses, so we can share ideas," she explains. "We spend one day per month together, have great speakers, and serve as advisory boards for each other." Ari, now a successful solo entrepreneur, has built a network of technical partners who share the same vision, collaborate, and funnel work to one another. He says that running a "client centered" business he believes in and working with people he respects have boosted his engagement tremendously.

Conclusion

Burnout can often feel insurmountable. But the sense of being overwhelmed is a signal, not a long-term sentence. By understanding the symptoms and causes and implementing these four strategies, you can recover and build a road map for prevention. Your brutal experience can serve as a turning point that launches you into a more sustainable career and a happier, healthier life.

———

Monique Valcour is an executive coach, keynote speaker, and management professor. She helps clients create and sustain fulfilling and high-performance jobs, careers, workplaces, and lives. Follow her on Twitter @moniquevalcour.

CHAPTER 8

Five Steps for Women to Combat Burnout

by Ellen Keithline Byrne

As an executive coach who works with women leaders, it's not unusual for me to see the sad, worried eyes of my coaching clients as the "aha" moment hits, and they realize: "I have burnout."

This realization often comes as a shock. Once it's teased out and women further share their feelings of exhaustion and lack of energy for work they once loved, it becomes glaringly obvious to them. But until that point, it's typically something they beat themselves up for,

Adapted from content posted on hbr.org, May 13, 2020 (product #H05JME).

their inner voice saying, "I just need to work harder! What's wrong with me?"

My business partners and I estimate that almost 20% of the women in our six-month leadership intensives are expressing some symptoms of burnout. What we know is that it's insidious and can slowly creep up on you. These clients have moved past periodic times of being "stressed out" into chronic stress. This occupational phenomenon clouds the mind, where a person struggles to assess their situation clearly, and they often end up beating themselves up for not being good enough.

One client, a CEO in a midsized insurance company, who had been truly passionate about her work, realized she was burned out. After years of tirelessly committing her time to the business, one day, she struggled to listen to the chairman of the board when he walked into her office, whereas in the past she looked forward to their conversations. She described it as the Charlie Brown adult voice that's just "wah, wah, wah." She felt exhausted when she woke up each morning, and just wanted to stay home, make soup, and watch *I Love Lucy* reruns.

This description is unfortunately not unusual. Our clients often have the reputation of being driven and passionate. Yet, over time, they feel overwhelmed and struggle to identify what's wrong. Sometimes, I hear them contemplate leaving their company just to find some sense of inner peace. And sometimes, they don't make changes until they end up in emergency rooms or with a serious health diagnosis. This can often lead to a leave of absence or termination. Successful leaders need to know what burnout looks like and get help early.

It's no surprise that women report higher levels of burnout. One study identified gender inequalities in the workplace as a key element that's impacting occupational mental health. Women were found to have lower levels of decision-making authority and were often over-qualified for their roles, which ultimately leads to less satisfaction at work and a sense that they have fewer career alternatives. We see this frustration all the time, and it often manifests in beating oneself up. Women often think it's their own fault that they're not thriving.

Our concern after decades of working with women leaders is that it's getting worse. Here is what we recommend.

Determine Right Away Whether You Have Burnout, and If So, How Bad It Is

Burnout is progressive. People typically start with one or two of the following identifiers, and it usually builds from there. Research by Christina Maslach and Michael Leiter (see chapter 24 of this guide) highlights three main questions to ask yourself:[1]

1. **Are you regularly physically and emotionally exhausted?** Do you feel a lack of energy and/or have trouble sleeping? Do you worry excessively? Feel more edgy? Feel sad or hopeless?

2. **Are you more cynical and detached than usual?** Do you no longer feel joy from things that used to bring you joy? Are you less interested in social-izing and are you feeling less connected to people

than you once did? Are you more negative than usual? Do you see the glass as half empty?

3. **Are you feeling like you're not contributing anything meaningful, where you once were?** Do you feel a sense of ineffectiveness and that all of your hard work isn't actually accomplishing anything?

If you respond yes to all or most of the questions, the alarm bells should be going off. It's time to schedule an appointment with your internist, mental health professional, or a coach. These questions—especially the last two—take the concept of normal "stress" to the next level, in terms of how it has impacted your overall mindset.

Catch It Early—Awareness Is the First Step

This is sometimes the hardest part. We can be tough on ourselves and are often not willing to reflect on our own behavior.

Clients will often share that colleagues and friends have expressed concern that they are not themselves or that they are doing too much. But they brush it off as just needing to work harder and smarter. If you're hearing similar comments from colleagues or friends, take heed. Coming to terms with the idea that you are either in "crisis" or heading there soon is not easy. Examine the list above and be honest with yourself.

Get Support

Whether a good friend, family member, therapist, or coach, it's important to have someone who can challenge your thinking and give you another perspective. Once burnout has its hold on your mindset, decision making can get fuzzy. By identifying patterns and regaining clarity on priorities, you can establish better boundaries, for instance, by delegating where necessary, by saying no to projects that do not serve you long term, and by taking better care of yourself. These steps can help you feel a sense of progress toward relieving your symptoms.

Make Your Emotional and Physical Well-Being a Priority

Put healthy eating, exercise, and a good sleep routine at the top of the list. Schedule in lunch breaks and stop working at a reasonable time. Take all of your vacation. Too many companies report that employees forgo vacation time; 27.2% of paid time off went unused in 2018. And too many women tell us that they're the first ones into the office, and the last ones out. Reframe that "work harder" message to work smarter, which includes breaks from work to stimulate the relaxation response and dissipate the stress response. It takes giving yourself permission to shift your mindset around what's a priority and a commitment to establishing healthy coping mechanisms to combat stress.

Examine Your Work Environment

Burnout is a result of a mismatch between the demands of the job and the available resources. In their HBR article "What's Really Holding Women Back" (March 2020), Robin Ely and Irene Padavic identified that "what holds women back at work is not some unique challenge of balancing the demands of work and family but rather a general problem of overwork that prevails in contemporary corporate culture." The current workplace mantra of "we have to do more with less" is not sustainable. With your manager or other senior leaders, review the structure of your role, the culture of the firm, and how to support an environment where everyone thrives.

For women leaders to better respond to and adapt to our changing workplaces, it's critical that a clearer understanding of what burnout is and how it manifests is necessary. As a coach, I hope that through education, my clients will be able to catch it early, apply the coping mechanisms they've learned, and not end up with serious health issues. We should all be striving for workplaces where everyone thrives.

––––––––––

Ellen Keithline Byrne is a cofounder of Her New Standard: The Playbook for Women Leaders, a leadership consulting firm focusing on advancing women in leadership, which designs boot camps for Women Leaders on the Rise. Find Ellen and her partners discussing strategies for women leaders on LinkedIn and Instagram.

NOTE

1. Christina Maslach and Michael Leiter, "Understanding the Burnout Experience: Recent Research and Its Implications for Psychiatry," *World Psychiatry* 15, no. 2 (2016): 103–111.

CHAPTER 9

Even If You Love Your Job, You May Need to Recharge

by Rebecca Knight

Even if you love your job, it's common to feel exhausted by it from time to time. It's not always full-on burnout. Perhaps you just wrapped up a big project and are having trouble mustering motivation for the next one. It could be that your home life is taking up more of your energy than usual. Or maybe you're just bored. Here are some quick ways to recharge.

Adapted from "How to Overcome Burnout and Stay Motivated," on hbr.org, April 2, 2015 (product #H01ZFC).

Take breaks during the workday

Burnout often stems from a "lack of understanding about what it takes to achieve peak workplace performance," says Ron Friedman, founder of the consulting firm ignite80 and the author of *The Best Place to Work: The Art and Science of Creating an Extraordinary Workplace.* "We tend to assume that [it] requires trying harder or outworking others, [which] may get you short-term results but [is] physiologically unsustainable." To perform at your best over the long term, you need regular "opportunities for restocking your mental energy," says Friedman. Take a walk or go for a run. Have lunch away from your desk. "Stepping away from your computer gets you out of the weeds and prompts you to reexamine the big picture," he advises.

Put away your digital devices

Before the smartphone era, leaving your work at the office was the default. "If you wanted to take work home with you, that required effort and planning," says Friedman. That's no longer the case. "Today we're all carrying around an office in our pocket in the form of a smartphone," so we're both psychologically and physiologically still attached. The remedy, he says, is to actively limit your use of digital devices after hours. Place your smartphone in a basket or drawer when you arrive home so you're not tempted to pick it up and check your email; or you might devise a rule for yourself about turning it off past 8 p.m.

Do something interesting

Instead of concentrating on limiting or avoiding work in your off-hours, Friedman recommends scheduling "restorative experiences that you look forward to." Making plans to play tennis with a friend or cook a meal with your spouse compels you to "focus on an *approach* goal—doing something pleasurable—instead of an *avoidance* goal—not checking email," he says.

Take long weekends

Feeling mentally and physically exhausted may also be a sign that "you need to take some time off," says Heidi Grant, a social psychologist and the author of *Reinforcements*. The break need not be a two-week vacation; rather, she says, when it comes to stress reduction, "you get a much greater benefit from regularly taking three- and four-day weekends." While you're away, though, don't call the office or check your email. "You need to let go," she says. "Each of us is a little less vital than we'd like to believe."

Focus on meaning

If your job responsibilities preclude immediate time off, Grant suggests "focusing on why the work matters to you." Connecting your current assignment to a larger personal goal—completing this project will help you score that next promotion, for instance—will "help you fight the temptation to slack off" and will provide a "jolt of energy that will give you what you need to barrel through that day or the next couple of days," she says.

Rebecca Knight is a freelance journalist in Boston and a lecturer at Wesleyan University. Her work has been published in the *New York Times, USA Today*, and the *Financial Times*.

CHAPTER 10

To Recover from Burnout, Regain Your Sense of Control

by Elizabeth Grace Saunders

You feel exhausted, ineffective, unaccomplished, and cynical. Maybe you feel as if no matter how hard you work, you can never keep up. Or that you can't make your boss happy no matter how hard you try. And you're beginning to question your professional situation: *Am I in the right job? The right company? The right career? I used to feel passionate about going into work but now*

Adapted from content posted on hbr.org, December 5, 2017 (product #H041JZ).

I dread Monday and can't wait until Friday. Will I ever feel excited about my life and work again?

These are classic signs that you're feeling burned out. And in that state, you often feel as if your circumstances are out of your control—as if everything around you is working against you. You might think: *Everyone else is to blame for my burnout.* But this victim mindset only blocks you from doing anything about your situation. While you're complaining about other people, the days of your life are ticking by.

It's far better to adopt an ownership mindset that sounds like this: *Others may have contributed to my situation, but I have the ability to make choices that can improve my present and future.* Thinking in this way gives you the license to choose, even in small ways, to take action to recharge and build momentum. Realizing you have autonomy opens up hope for the future.

Next, you can choose to believe that the right actions will lead to the right feelings, rather than the other way around. When you're in a burnout state, it's easy to think that no matter what you do, it won't make a difference. This is because of actual physiological changes to your brain that cause you to take less interest in activities that would otherwise make you happy.[1] To fight against this negativity, remind yourself you don't need to feel like taking action in order to do so. In fact, taking action leads to a higher desire to do more positive activities in the future.

Then, increase your attentiveness to your body's physical and emotional needs. It could be as simple as getting up to stretch your legs when you're feeling stiff, eating lunch with coworkers instead of at your desk, or going to bed when you're tired. If you're in a state of burnout, you will need more sleep than usual; it's part of your body's healing process. You also will need breaks throughout the day. Breaks are beneficial for anyone—they help restore your energy—but they're especially important if you're burned out, in part because making the choice to take them demonstrates to yourself that you have some level of control, even on a micro level.

Finally, question your assumptions about the way that your work life *has* to be and what you *have* to do. I really like how Jason Fried, cofounder and CEO of Basecamp, put it in this *Hurry, Slowly* podcast interview: "Just because a company pays you doesn't mean they own you."

Who says that you can't leave work at work tonight? Or ask for a deadline extension? Can you take yourself off that committee, or take a real vacation? Often you have a lot more choice than you believe. You need to test the perceived limits to discover what could improve in your situation.

I recommend starting small, especially if you feel hesitant. For example, you could decide that at least one weeknight, you won't take any work home. Or after a certain time each night, you'll disconnect from your devices. Small steps like these lower the risk on your end and allows others to gradually adjust to your new relationship with work.

At first, you may not need to talk directly with your colleagues about the changes. But in time, you'll likely want and need to open up. Perhaps you have a conversation with your boss to discuss which projects are the highest priority for this quarter and which can wait. Or you work with your colleagues on sharing responsibilities on a project or even bringing in more resources.

And if you're in a professional position where people really do have unreasonable demands and you can't set boundaries, think bigger. Consider looking for a new job, or even a new career. These changes likely will take time. But it's good to remember that the choice is there. Life doesn't have to be the way that it's always been. Changing your mindset and taking small actions will help you begin the process of feeling less burned out and more hopeful about the future.

———————

Elizabeth Grace Saunders is a time management coach and the founder of Real Life E Time Coaching & Speaking. She is author of *How to Invest Your Time Like Money* and *Divine Time Management*. Find out more at www.RealLifeE.com.

NOTE

1. Alexandra Michel, "Burnout and the Brain," Association for Physical Science, January 29, 2016, https://www.psychologicalscience.org/observer/burnout-and-the-brain.

CHAPTER 11

Instead of Pushing Yourself Too Hard, Help Others Around You Perform

by Merete Wedell-Wedellsborg

As we begin our coaching session, Nick is fired up. He radiates energy, his eyes are beaming with determination, and he never really comes to a full rest. He speaks passionately of a new initiative he is spearheading, taking

Adapted from "Help Your Team Do More Without Burning Out," on hbr.org, October 15, 2018 (product #H04L4E).

on the looming threats from Silicon Valley, and rethinking his company's business model completely.

I recognize this behavior in Nick, having seen it many times over the years since he was first singled out as a high-potential talent. "Restless and relentless" have been his trademarks as he has risen through the ranks and aced one challenge after another.

But this time, I notice something new. Beneath the usual can-do attitude, there is an inkling of something else: mild disorientation and even signs of exhaustion. "It's like sprinting all you can, and then you turn a corner and find that you are actually setting out on a marathon," he remarks at one point. And as we speak, this sneaking feeling of not keeping pace turns out to be Nick's true concern: Is he about to lose his magic touch and burn out?

Nick is not alone.

In a psychologist's practice, common themes rise and wane across a cohort of clients. Right now, I see a surge of concern about speed: getting ahead and *staying* ahead. More clients use similar metaphors about "running to stand still" or feeling "caught on a track." Invariably, their first response is to speed up and run faster.

But the impulse to simply run faster to escape friction is obviously of no use for the long haul of a lifelong career. In fact, our immediate behavioral response to friction shares one feature with much of the general advice about speeding up: It is plainly counterproductive and leads to burnout rather than breakout.

To add insult to injury, the way to wrestle effectively with the challenge of *sustainable speed* is somewhat counterintuitive and even disconcerting—especially to high-performing leaders who have successfully relied on their personal drive to make results.

From Ego-Drive to Co-Drive

The key to speeding up without burning up is a concept I call *co-drive*. Sustainable speed does not come from ego-drive, that is, your own personal performance or energy level, but rather from a different approach to engaging with people around you.

Rather than running faster, Nick needs to make different moves altogether. First, he must let go of his obsession with his own development, his own needs, his own performance, and his own pace. Second, he must start obsessing about other people.

It may seem illogical, but the leap to a new growth curve begins by realizing that the recipe is not to take on more and speed up, but to slow down and let go of some of the issues that have been your driving forces: power, prestige, responsibility, recognition, or face time.

The talent phase in our careers tends to be profoundly self-centered, even narcissistic. If you need to move on from the first growth curve in your career and want to take on more challenges, you need to exchange ego-drive for co-drive.

Co-drive requires that you momentarily forget yourself—and instead focus on others. The shift involves an understanding that you have *already* proven yourself.

At this stage, the point is to help those around you perform. The change to co-drive involves moving from a stage of grabbing territory to a stage characterized by letting go of command and control.

Beyond Teamwork

So here is what Nick needs to do: Rather than striving to be energetic, he should aim to be energizing. Rather than setting the pace, he should aspire to make teams self-propelling. Instead of delegating tasks, he should learn to lead by congregating.

Be energizing, not energetic

Here is the paradox: You can actually speed things up by slowing down. There is no doubt that being energetic is contagious and therefore a short-term source of momentum. But if you lead by example all the time, your batteries will eventually run dry. You risk being drained at the very point when your leadership is needed the most. Conveying a sense of urgency is useful, but an excess of urgency suffocates team development and reflection at the very point it is needed. "Code red" should be left for real emergencies.

Nick has always had a weak point for people who, like himself, are high energy and get things done. These "Energizer Bunnies" are his star players. However, with the co-drive mindset, Nick needs to widen his sights and recognize and reward people who are good at energizing others. Energizing behavior is unselfish and generous, and praises, not just progress, but personality too.

Seek self-propulsion, not pace setting

If you lead by beating the drum, setting tight deadlines, and burning the midnight oil, your team becomes overly dependent on your presence. Sustainable speed is achievable only if the team propels itself without your presence. Jim Collins, author of *Good to Great*, wrote that great leaders don't waste time telling time; they build clocks.

Self-propulsion comes from letting go of control, resisting the urge to make detailed corrections and allowing for informal leadership to flourish. As Harvard Kennedy School professor Ron Heifetz advocates, true leadership is realizing that you need to "give the work back" instead of being the hero who sweeps in and solves everybody's problems.

In Nick's case, he should resist the urge to take the driver's seat and allow himself to take the passenger seat instead. Leading from the sideline, not the front line, will change his perspective. Instead of looking at the road and navigating traffic, he is able to monitor how the driver is actually doing and what needs to improve. In his mind, he should fire himself—momentarily—and see what happens to his team when he sets them free and asks them to take charge instead of looking to him for answers, deadlines, and decisions.

Congregate, don't delegate

From very early on in our careers, we learn that in order to solve big, complex issues fast, we must decompose the problem into smaller parts and delegate these pieces to specialists to get leverage. Surely, you can make good music by patching together the tracks of individual recordings. But true masterpieces come alive when the orchestra plays together.

One example is the so-called Trauma Center approach. When a trauma patient comes in, all specialists are in the room assessing the patient at the same time, but constantly allowing the most skilled specialist to take the lead (and talk), not the designated leader.

The most well-run trauma teams I have observed know when to jump in and when to step back. To put it simply, it's no use working on a finger if the heart is failing. A trauma team relies on trust and patience. They trust each other's specialty and work very symmetrically. There is a very strong "no one leaves before we are done" mentality in those teams.

To Nick, this may sound like good old teamwork, and while Nick is certainly driven by a good measure of self-interest, he is also an accomplished leader who masters the dynamics of teamwork: having shared goals, assigning roles and responsibilities, and investing in the team.

But there is more to co-drive than plain teamwork. It is about reworking the collaborative process itself. Rather than siloed problem solving, sustainable speed requires a shift toward more collective creation: gathering often, engaging issues openly and inviting others to *improve* on your own thoughts and decisions.

Co-drive requires a different mindset. And it goes beyond teamwork. Adam Grant from Wharton has done research demonstrating that a generous and giving attitude toward others enhances team performance.

Try, for instance, to take a look at your own behavior yesterday and gauge the balance between giving and taking. Givers offer assistance, share knowledge, and focus on introducing and helping others. Takers attempt to get other people to do something that will ultimately benefit them, while they act as gatekeepers of their own knowledge.

Grant's conclusion is clear: A willingness to help others is not just the essence of effective cooperation and innovation—it is also the key to accelerating your own performance.

Maturity and Caliber

Headhunters call this change of perspective from ego-drive to co-drive "executive maturity." The mature leader's burning question is: How do I help *others* perform?

The developmental psychologist Robert Kegan calls the leap a subject/object shift. You progress from seeing and navigating in the world on the basis of your own needs and motives—and allowing yourself to be governed by these needs—to seeing yourself from an external position as a part of an organism.

It requires a certain caliber and self-assuredness to act in this way. The ability to put your ego on hold may require a great effort. It might be worthwhile reminding yourself of the words of the American President Harry Truman: "It is incredible what you can achieve, if you don't care who gets the credit." If you succeed in making this shift, and thereby improving the skills of the people around you, then you will also experience a greater degree of freedom.

So next time you are feeling stuck, don't ask: "How can I push harder?" but "Where can I let go?"

_____

Merete Wedell-Wedellsborg works as an executive adviser to senior-level leaders and teams. She has practiced clinical psychology and has worked extensively in the financial sector. She is the author of *Battle Mind: Performing Under Pressure* and holds a PhD in business economics and an MA in organizational psychology.

CHAPTER 12

Carve a New Path at Work

by Jennifer Moss

As leaders look for new ways to improve workplace well-being while reducing stress and burnout, a relatively new concept has emerged: job crafting, a strategy that gives employees the chance to design their roles for a more meaningful experience of work.

Scientists have found that monotonous work can negatively impact mental health, cause us major stress, and lead to burnout. The chronically bored are at higher risk for drug addiction, alcoholism, and compulsive gambling. In her paper, "Neuroscience Reveals That Boredom Hurts," Dr. Judy Willis, a neurologist and former

---

Adapted from "If You're Burning Out, Carve a New Path," on hbr.org, April 1, 2020 (product #H05IOE).

classroom teacher, claims that when we're bored, our judgment, goal-directed planning, risk assessment, focus, and control over our emotions all suffer.[1] And a Korn Ferry poll of nearly 5,000 professionals claims that the top reason people look for a new job is boredom.[2]

Meaning and Mental Health at Work

Monotony, lack of flow, and a lack of autonomy have all been shown to increase stress and burnout in the workplace.

Richard Thackray, from the Washington, DC, Office of Aviation Medicine, wanted to understand the dangers for pilots if there was too much automation and boredom in their roles. In his paper, "The Stress of Boredom and Monotony," he acknowledges that workplace monotony has already been shown to adversely impact morale, performance, and quality of work.[3] However, his laboratory and field studies show that the combination of tasks that feel monotonous and lack meaning with deadline-driven roles and fast-paced work environments is a recipe for burnout.

Dr. Shahram Heshmat, an associate professor emeritus at the University of Illinois at Springfield, claims workplace monotony can be caused by:

1. Experiences that are repetitive and predictable, especially when we lack interest in the details of our tasks.

2. A lack of "flow"—a term coined by Mihály Csíkszentmihályi in 1975, defined as a state of

total immersion in a task that is challenging, yet closely matched to one's abilities, often referred to as "being in the zone." Tasks that are too easy lack meaning and become tedious.

3. Work experiences that stop feeling novel. Novel experiences pump chemicals like dopamine into our brains, which is strongly linked to motivation and reward seeking. At work, it helps us meet deadlines, reach goals, and enjoy the work that we do every day. Conversely, once the brain identifies an experience as familiar, it stops seeking rewards and loses its potential to motivate. Novelty is so important to well-being that researchers claim that it's a predictor of longevity.

4. The belief that we lack agency or autonomy (the ability to make choices about how we work, what we work on, with whom we work, etc.). Autonomy in the workplace refers to how much personal freedom employees have to make decisions. This can range from schedule setting, to how goals are met, to what type of work we do from one day to the next. Higher levels of autonomy tend to result in an increase in job satisfaction, while lower levels of autonomy increase stress and can lead to burnout.[4]

The above research clearly indicates that a lack of meaning in our work, limited agency over how we achieve our goals, and insufficient novelty in the tasks we engage in every day can have serious negative impacts on our mental and physical health. Job crafting may be exactly what leaders need as an antidote to these workplace stressors.

Replacing Boredom with Meaning

The reality is, most employees are required to carry out similar or identical tasks every day. It's challenging to avoid repetitive work, even when we enjoy what we do. In general, humans are attracted to repetition. Studies show that about 40% of our daily activities are performed each day in almost the same situations.[5] Subconscious behaviors allow our conscious brain to be more mindful and feel more psychologically safe. The trade-off for the comfort of routine can mean a less enjoyable experience when we engage in these tasks.

So, what if we could make small tweaks to how we perform those actions, or change the way we perceive these tasks, so they stop feeling monotonous and instead feel novel and purposeful? This is the magic of job crafting. It transforms parts of our work that once felt meaningless into something that feels valued.

In 2001, Jane Dutton, professor emerita of business administration and psychology at the University of Michigan, and Amy Wrzesniewski, professor of management at Yale, conceptualized the idea of job crafting. They define it as a means of describing the ways in which employees utilize opportunities to customize their jobs by actively changing their tasks and interactions with others at work. The main idea is that we can stay in the same role, getting more meaning out of our jobs simply by changing what we do and the purpose behind it. Imagine you are a secretary at a public school. You can either think of your job as someone who writes late slips and calls parents when their children are absent or see yourself as an essential liaison between families, student, and school staff. You create the right environment for students to thrive by ensuring their safety and managing communication for them so they are supported at home.

Job crafting gives you the space to go beyond the job description and shape a meaning for the work you do. Managers shouldn't expect that repetitive tasks will no longer get accomplished, but these types of tasks don't define the role.

The Benefits of Job Crafting to Avoid Burnout

As an author, my role is in a constant state of job crafting. When I'm writing, I get into a complete state of flow. Sounds stop permeating. The external world ceases to exist. On the flip side, research can feel tedious. For every 10 academic journals I read, I may get one significant piece of data that may or may not remain in the piece. It's like I'm mining for gold. Since I care deeply about evidence-based writing, this process is necessary. It is also a significant part of an author's daily work experience, definitely "part of the job."

I realized that if I wanted to enjoy the flow I feel while writing, I needed to change how I perceive the task of researching. I started by jotting down a short list of why evidence-based writing is so important to me. First, it backs up opinions with facts. Second, it relies on experts who have a deeper knowledge of the subject matter at hand than most. Finally, it provides us all with novel information that provokes new thinking. This list kick-started an "ideas bucket" for me, and every cool fact or interesting data point or thought-provoking case study would find its way there. These ideas have helped me exponentially as future stories came into view. They push me to learn new things and experience all the thrilling chemistry that comes with novel experiences in the brain. It also increases my energy, reduces monotony, and prevents me from burning out.

Dutton, Wrzesniewksi, and Gelaye Debebe, associate professor of organizational sciences at George Washington University, coauthored the paper, "Being Valued and Devalued at Work: A Social Valuing Perspective," where they analyze the impact of job crafting as it relates to meaning and perception of role value.[6] The study examined cleaners at a prestigious university hospital known for its high-tech medicine. Although the cleaners in the study were more or less doing the same job, each one described their experience uniquely. The subjects were broken out into two groups—those who enjoyed their jobs, and those who did not. The group that didn't enjoy their roles described their jobs as if they were reading a job description—required tasks only. They also described their work as requiring low skill and said that people didn't notice them.

Cleaners who enjoyed their work included details like interacting with patients and visitors in their job descriptions, and believed their work was of high value. They also referred to themselves as "ambassadors and healers," and would seek out assignments to support that self-title—such as spending more time with patients who seemed lonely, or regularly changing the pictures on the walls where patients were comatose to make the room feel nicer, so it might just help them revive.

In a discussion with Shankar Vedantam, on NPR's You 2.0., Amy Wrzesniewksi further elaborated on her interviews with the cleaners.[7] She shared that the employees who enjoyed their jobs also behaved with empathy toward the patients, as if they were family. In one scenario, Wrzesniewksi describes how cleaning staff would put themselves in the physical place of a patient by looking up toward the ceiling "to see if there were things that were up there that we might not notice, but would bother the patients if they had to look at them all day long."

Purpose-driven roles are some of the most vulnerable to burnout and therefore require us to be mindful that we don't take job crafting too far. By adding new dimensions to our roles, we may increase passion, but we also run the risk of carrying an increased workload and suffering from exhaustion. Leadership should be reminded that autonomy and meaning are valuable to employees and tend to produce higher levels of engagement and happiness at work. However, managers still need to check in and remain accountable to how their employees are keeping those two forces in balance, so they don't end up getting burned out.

For organizations looking to retain their top talent, it's important to understand that boredom is kryptonite for high performers and inspiration-seeking millennials.

Leaders would benefit from giving employees the autonomy to increase purpose and meaning in their roles and reduce the repetitive tasks that fuel chronic stress and burnout. Not only does this prevent the potential for burnout, but it increases productivity, engagement, and retention. Best of all, job crafting can give us all a reason to look up.

———

Jennifer Moss is an award-winning journalist, author, and international public speaker. She is a CBC Radio Columnist, reporting on topics related to happiness and well-being. She contributes regularly to *Harvard Business Review* and writes for the Society of Human Resource Management (SHRM). She sits on the Global Happiness Council in support of the UN's Sustainable Development Goals related to well-being. Her book *Unlocking Happiness at Work* was named Business Book of the Year and her forthcoming book on burnout will be published by Harvard Business Review Press.

NOTES

1. Judy Willis, "Neuroscience Reveals That Boredom Hurts," *Phi Delta Kappan* 95, no. 8 (2014).

2. Gary Burnison, "Breaking Boredom: What's Really Driving Job Seekers in 2018," Korn Ferry, 2018, https://www.kornferry.com/insights/articles/job-hunting-2018-boredom.

3. R. I. Thackray, "The Stress of Boredom and Monotony: A Consideration of the Evidence," *Psychosomatic Medicine* 43, no. 2 (1981): 165–176.

4. Shahram Heshmat, "Eight Reasons Why We Get Bored," *Psychology Today*, June 16, 2017.

5. Society for Personality and Social Psychology, "How We Form Habits, Change Existing Ones," *ScienceDaily*, August 8, 2014, https://www.sciencedaily.com/releases/2014/08/140808111931.htm.

6. Jane Dutton, Amy Wrzesniewksi, and Gelaye Debebe, "Being Valued and Devalued at Work: A Social Valuing Perspective," *Qualitative Organizational Research: Best Papers from the Davis Conference on Qualitative Research*, vol. 3, Information Age Publishing, 2012, http://webuser.bus.umich.edu/janedut/High%20Quality%20 Connections/Being%20valued%20%20final.pdf.

7. Shankar Vedantam, "You 2.0: Dream Jobs," *Hidden Brain*, NPR, July 30, 2018, https://www.npr.org/transcripts/634047154?story Id=634047154?storyId=634047154.

CHAPTER 13

When Burnout Is a Sign You Should Leave Your Job

by Monique Valcour

You have the right to have work that enriches and enlivens you, rather than diminishing you. This is my own personal declaration of human rights at work. It informs everything I do as a coach, management professor, and human being. Yet it's surprisingly controversial. Managers and employees in organizations around the world have bought into the assumption that pay and other contracted rewards are all you can expect to receive from work (and all that you owe your employees) and that it's

Adapted from content posted on hbr.org, January 25, 2018 (product #H044KG).

unrealistic to hope for less-tangible benefits like trust, respect, autonomy, civility, and the opportunity to make a positive impact on others. This impoverished view of work plays out in workplace attitudes and behaviors that burn employees out. It also traps people in jobs that harm their well-being and sense of self.

When the conditions and demands you encounter at work—like workload, level of autonomy, and norms of interpersonal behavior—exceed your capacity to handle them, you're at risk of burning out. Burnout has three components: exhaustion (lost energy), cynicism (lost enthusiasm), and inefficacy (lost self-confidence and capacity to perform), but you don't have to be experiencing all three in order to suffer serious consequences (see chapter 7 of this guide). For example, if you don't believe in your organization's core activities, leadership, and culture, you're likely to feel demoralized even if you still function well at work.

While research has established that job and organizational factors that are largely outside of an individual employee's control contribute to burnout at least as much as personal factors, attempts to reduce or prevent burnout primarily fall to individuals. Therefore, there may come a time when leaving your job or organization is the best possible course of action in response to burnout. I faced this decision a few years ago while working for an organization that had numerous burnout risk factors and many burned-out employees. I tried multiple strategies to increase my engagement, such as crafting my job (see chapter 12 of this guide). I looked for ways to create value for my employer that exploited my strengths.

I gained agreement for slight job modifications that allowed me to spend more time on work I found meaningful and less time on assignments I disliked. I reduced my exposure to tasks, people, and situations that drained my energy to the extent that I could.

Over time, however, my ability to exert control over my job was significantly constrained. I was assigned a higher load of stressful assignments and denied the opportunity to take on those I found fulfilling. Vigorous exercise, yoga, and meditation proved inadequate to control my stress; I found it necessary to take tranquilizers as well. I was unable to achieve any psychological distance from the stresses of my workplace. Familiar tasks required greater time and effort to complete, with the result that I worked nearly continuously. I've always been achievement-oriented, so feeling my creative and productive capacity draining away from me was frightening. Friends observed that I was clearly miserable at work. I came to realize that even though leaving my job might entail a major career change and an unwelcome relocation, my well-being depended on it.

If you're feeling burned out, how do you know when it's time to call it quits? Reflecting on the following questions can help you to determine whether you should leave your job.

Does Your Job/Employer Enable You to Be the Best Version of Yourself?

A sustainable job leverages your strengths and helps you perform at your peak. One of the most consistently demoralizing experiences my coaching clients report is having to work in conditions that constrain their performance to a level well below their potential—for example, overwhelming workload, conflicting objectives, unclear expectations, inadequate resources, and lack of managerial support. Persistent barriers to good performance thwart the human need for mastery. Furthermore, when you're burned out, you provide less value than you would working in conditions that are more conducive to your performance and engagement. As my burnout progressed, my motivation plummeted and I had less to offer my employer. Not only was the organization hurting me, I was hurting the organization. Burnout is like a relationship that's gone bad: When the employment relationship is no longer beneficial to either party and the prospects for reviving it are dim, it may be time to call it quits.

How Well Does Your Job/Employer Align with Your Values and Interests?

When you experience a sense of fit between your values and interests and the values and needs of your organization, you are more likely to find meaning and purpose in your work. When fit is bad, on the other hand, you probably won't receive the support you need to perform well. Your career success suffers. My employer's values as revealed by managerial behavior and decision-making practices clashed with my core commitments to authenticity, autonomy, making a positive difference, and facilitating thriving at work. While there were small ways in which I could create value, help others, and enjoy moments of satisfaction, overall, the landscape appeared bleak. I reasoned that rather than trying to garden in a desert, I'd be better off seeking fertile soil elsewhere to cultivate the fruits I longed to bring to life.

What Does Your Future Look Like in Your Job/Organization?

Zoom out and take a long-term perspective to assess whether you've hit a short-term rough patch or a long-term downward slide. Do you recognize yourself in senior members of the organization? Do they give you a hopeful vision of your future? The possibility of living out the reality that some of my senior colleagues were living filled me with dread. Considering a few senior colleagues who were clearly diminished by their employment, frequently sick, and consistently negative set off alarm bells for me. I knew that I didn't want to end up like that. Opportunities to expand into new areas and develop skills I hoped to build appeared slim. My future in the organization was one of stagnation.

What Is Burnout Costing You?

Burnout can take a serious toll on your health, performance, career prospects, psychological well-being, and relationships. In my case, the negative emotions I brought home hurt my marriage and family relationships as well as my peace of mind. Sitting in the office of a relationship counselor and hearing my always supportive husband say, "I have no more empathy left for you," clarified the costs of burnout on me and my family.

If you're unsure about the impact that burnout might be having on you, try asking your partner, family members, and close friends for their perspective.

After considering these questions, if you conclude that leaving your job or organization is the right course of action for you, you've already turned a corner. You may not be able to quit today. But maybe today is the day that you begin to lay the groundwork: Put aside extra savings, update your résumé, reach out to network contacts, spread the word that you'd like a new job, get a coach, or sign up for an online course. The journey back to thriving begins with actions like these. In my case, I began lining up side gigs, got certified as a coach, and negotiated some additional training support as part of a separation agreement with my employer. I built a portfolio of fulfilling work activities into a sustainable career that I love. I'm convinced that if meaningful, rewarding work matters to you and if you commit to achieving it, you are more likely to enjoy your right to enriching work.

Monique Valcour is an executive coach, keynote speaker, and management professor. She helps clients create and sustain fulfilling and high-performance jobs, careers, workplaces, and lives. Follow her on Twitter @moniquevalcour.

CHAPTER 14

Reawakening Your Passion for Work

by Richard Boyatzis, Annie McKee, and Daniel Goleman

"Am I really living the way I want to live?" We all struggle with the question of personal meaning throughout our lives. The senior executives who read *Harvard Business Review*, for instance, seem to struggle with this question at the high point of their careers. Why? Many executives hit their professional stride in their forties and fifties, just as their parents are reaching the end of their lives—a reminder that all of us are mortal. What's more, many of the personality traits associated with career success, such as a knack for problem solving and sheer tenacity, lead people to stick with a difficult situation in the hope

Adapted from an article in *Harvard Business Review*, April 2002 (product #R0204G).

of making it better. Then one day, a creeping sensation sets in: Something is wrong. That realization launches a process we have witnessed—literally thousands of times—in our work coaching managers and executives over the past 14 years.

The process is rarely easy, but we've found this type of awakening to be healthy and necessary; leaders need to go through it every few years to replenish their energy, creativity, and commitment—and to rediscover their passion for work and life. Indeed, leaders cannot keep achieving new goals and inspiring the people around them without understanding their own dreams. In this article, we'll look at the different signals that it's time to take stock—whether you have a nagging sense of doubt that builds over time until it's impossible to ignore or you experience a life-changing event that irrevocably alters your perspective. Then we'll describe some strategies for listening to those signals and taking restorative action. Such action can range from a relatively minor adjustment in outlook, to a larger refocusing on what really matters, to practical life changes that take you in an entirely new direction.

When to Say When

When asked, most businesspeople say that passion— to lead, to serve the customer, to support a cause or a product—is what drives them. When that passion fades, they begin to question the meaning of their work. How can you reawaken the passion and reconnect with what's meaningful for you? The first step is acknowledging the signal that it's time to take stock. Let's look at the various feelings that let you know the time has come.

"I feel trapped."

Sometimes, a job that was fulfilling gradually becomes less meaningful, slowly eroding your enthusiasm and spirit until you no longer find much purpose in your work. People often describe this state as feeling trapped. They're restless, yet they can't seem to change—or even articulate what's wrong.

Take the case of Bob McDowell, the corporate director of human resources at a large professional-services firm. After pouring his heart and soul into his work for 25 years, Bob had become terribly demoralized because his innovative programs were cut time and again. As a result, his efforts could do little to improve the workplace over the long term. For years he had quieted his nagging doubts, in part because an occasional success or a rare employee who flourished under his guidance provided deep, if temporary, satisfaction. Moreover, the job carried all the usual trappings of success—title, money, and perks. And, like most people in middle age, McDowell had financial responsibilities that made it risky to trade security for personal fulfillment. Factors such as these conspire to keep people trudging along, hoping things will get better. But clinging to security or trying to be a good corporate citizen can turn out to be a prison of your own making.

"I'm bored."

Many people confuse achieving day-to-day business goals with performing truly satisfying work, so they continue setting and achieving new goals—until it dawns on them that they are bored. People are often truly shaken by this revelation; they feel as if they have just emerged from a spiritual blackout. We saw this in Nick Mimken, the owner of a successful insurance agency, who increasingly felt that something was missing from his life. He joined a book group, hoping that intellectual stimulation would help him regain some enthusiasm, but it wasn't enough. The fact was, he had lost touch with his dreams and was going through the motions at work without experiencing any real satisfaction from the success of his business.

High achievers like Mimken may have trouble accepting that they're bored because it's often the generally positive traits of ambition and determination to succeed that obscure the need for fun. Some people may feel guilty about being restless when it looks like they have it all. Others may admit they aren't having fun but believe that's the price of success. As one manager said, "I work to live. I don't expect to find deep meaning at the office; I get that elsewhere." The problem? Like many, this man works more than 60 hours a week, leaving him little time to enjoy anything else.

"I'm not the person I want to be."

Some people gradually adjust to the letdowns, frustrations, and even boredom of their work until they surrender to a routine that's incompatible with who they are and what they truly want. Consider, for instance, John Lauer, an inspirational leader who took over as president of BFGoodrich and quickly captured the support of top executives with his insight into the company's challenges and opportunities and his contagious passion for the business.

But after he'd been with the company about six years, we watched Lauer give a speech to a class of executive MBA students and saw that he had lost his spark. Over time, Lauer had fallen in step with a corporate culture that was focused on shareholder value in a way that was inconsistent with what he cared about. Not surprisingly, he left the company six months later, breaking from corporate life by joining his wife in her work with Hungarian relief organizations. He later admitted that he knew he wasn't himself by the end of his time at BFGoodrich, although he didn't quite know why.

How did Lauer stray from his core? First, the change was so gradual that he didn't notice that he was being absorbed into a culture that didn't fit him. Second, like many, he did what he felt he "should," going along with the bureaucracy and making minor concession after minor concession rather than following his heart. Finally, he exhibited a trait that is a hallmark of effective leaders: adaptability. At first, adapting to the corporate culture probably made Lauer feel more comfortable. But without strong self-awareness, people risk adapting to such an extent that they no longer recognize themselves.

"I won't compromise my ethics."

The signal to take stock may come to people in the form of a challenge to what they feel is right. Such was the case for Niall FitzGerald, former cochairman of Unilever, when he was asked to take a leadership role in South Africa, which was still operating under apartheid. The offer was widely considered a feather in his cap and a positive sign about his future with Unilever. Until that time, FitzGerald had accepted nearly every assignment, but the South Africa opportunity stopped him in his tracks, posing a direct challenge to his principles. How could he, in good conscience, accept a job in a country whose political and practical environment he found reprehensible?

Or consider the case of a manager we'll call Rob. After working for several supportive and loyal bosses, he found himself reporting to an executive—we'll call him Martin—whose management style was in direct conflict with Rob's values. The man's abusive treatment of subordinates had derailed a number of promising careers, yet he was something of a legend in the company. To Rob's chagrin, the senior executive team admired Martin's performance and, frankly, felt that young managers benefited from a stint under his marine lieutenant–style leadership.

When you recognize that an experience is in conflict with your values, as FitzGerald and Rob did, you can at least make a conscious choice about how to respond. The problem is, people often miss this particular signal because they lose sight of their core values. Sometimes they separate their work from their personal lives to such an extent that they don't bring their values to the office. As a result, they may accept or even engage in behaviors they'd deem unacceptable at home. Other people find that their work *becomes* their life, and business goals take precedence over everything else. Many executives who genuinely value family above all still end up working 12-hour days, missing more and more family dinners as they pursue success at work. In these cases, people may not hear the wake-up call. Even if they do, they may sense that something isn't quite right but be unable to identify it—or do anything to change it.

"I can't ignore the call."

A wake-up call can come in the form of a mission: an irresistible force that compels people to step out, step up, and take on a challenge. It is as if they suddenly recognize what they are meant to do and cannot ignore it any longer.

Such a call is often spiritual, as in the case of the executive who, after examining his values and personal vision, decided to quit his job, become ordained, buy a building, and start a church—all at age 55. But a call can take other forms as well—to become a teacher, to work with disadvantaged children, or to make a difference to the people you encounter every day. Rebecca Yoon, who runs a dry-cleaning business, has come to consider it her mission to connect with her customers on a personal level. Her constant and sincere attention has created remarkable loyalty to her shop, even though the actual service she provides is identical to that delivered by hundreds of other dry cleaners in the city.

"Life is too short!"

Sometimes it takes a trauma, large or small, to jolt people into taking a hard look at their lives. Such an awakening may be the result of a heart attack, the loss of a loved one, or a world tragedy. It can also be the result of something less dramatic, like adjusting to an empty nest or celebrating a significant birthday. Priorities can become crystal clear at times like these, and things that seemed important weeks, days, or even minutes ago no longer matter.

For example, following a grueling and heroic escape from his office at One World Trade Center on September 11, 2001, John Paul DeVito of the May Davis Group stumbled into a church in tears, desperate to call his family. When a police officer tried to calm him down, DeVito responded, "I'm not in shock. I've never been more cognizant in my life." Even as he mourned the deaths of friends and colleagues, he continued to be ecstatic about life, and he's now reframing his priorities, amazed that before this horrific experience he put duty to his job above almost everything else.

DeVito is not alone. Anecdotal evidence suggests that many people felt the need to seek new meaning in their lives after the tragedies of 9/11, which highlighted the fact that life can be cut short at any time. An article in the December 26, 2001, *Wall Street Journal* described two women who made dramatic changes after the attacks. Following a visit to New York shortly after the towers were hit, engineer Betty Roberts quit her job at age 52 to enroll in divinity school. And Chicki Wentworth decided to give up the office and restaurant building she had owned and managed for nearly 30 years in order to work with troubled teens.

But as we've said, people also confront awakening events throughout their lives in much more mundane circumstances. Turning 40, getting married, sending a child to college, undergoing surgery, facing retirement—these are just a handful of the moments in life when we naturally pause, consider where our choices have taken us, and check our accomplishments against our dreams.

Interestingly, it's somehow more socially acceptable to respond to shocking or traumatic events than to any of the others. As a result, people who feel trapped and bored often stick with a job that's making them miserable for far too long, and thus they may be more susceptible to stress-related illnesses. What's more, the quieter signals—a sense of unease that builds over time, for example—can be easy to miss or dismiss because their day-to-day impact is incremental. But such signals are no less important as indicators of the need to reassess than the more visible events. How do you learn to listen to vital signals and respond before it's too late? It takes a conscious, disciplined effort at periodic self-examination.

Strategies for Renewal

There's no one-size-fits-all solution for restoring meaning and passion to your life. However, there are strategies for assessing your life and making corrections if you've gotten off course. Most people pursue not a single strategy but a combination, and some seek outside help while others prefer a more solitary journey. Regardless of which path you choose, you need time for reflection—a chance to consider where you are, where you're going, and where you really want to be. Let's look at five approaches.

Call a time-out

For some people, taking time off is the best way to figure out what they really want to do and to reconnect with their dreams. Academic institutions have long provided time for rejuvenation through sabbaticals—six to 12 months off, often with pay. Some businesses—to be clear, very few—offer sabbaticals as well, letting people take a paid leave to pursue their interests with the guarantee of a job when they return. More often, businesspeople who take time off do so on their own time—a risk, to be sure, but few who have stepped off the track regret the decision.

This is the path Bob McDowell took. McDowell, the HR director we described earlier who felt trapped in his job, stepped down from his position, did not look for another job, and spent about eight months taking stock of his life. He considered his successes and failures and faced up to the sacrifices he had made by dedicating himself so completely to a job that was, in the end, less than fulfilling. Other executives take time off with far less ambitious goals—simply to get their heads out of their work for a while and focus on their personal lives. After a time, they may very happily go back to the work they'd been doing for years, eager to embrace the same challenges with renewed passion.

Still others might want to step off the fast track and give their minds a rest by doing something different. When Nick Mimken, the bored head of an insurance agency, took stock of his life and finally realized he wasn't inspired by his work, he decided to sell his business, keep only a few clients, and take sculpture classes. He then went to work as a day laborer for a landscaper in order to pursue his interest in outdoor sculpture—in particular, stone fountains. Today he and his wife live in Nantucket, Massachusetts, where he no longer works *for* a living but *at* living. He is exploring what speaks to him—be it rock sculpture, bronze casting, protecting wildlife, or teaching people how to handle their money. Nick is deeply passionate about his work and how he is living his life. He calls himself a life explorer.

In any event, whether it's an intense soul-searching exercise or simply a break from corporate life, people almost invariably find time-outs energizing. But stepping out isn't easy. No to-do lists, no meetings or phone calls, no structure—it can be difficult for high achievers to abandon their routines. The loss of financial security makes this move inconceivable for some. And for the many people whose identities are tied up in their professional lives, walking away feels like too great a sacrifice. Indeed, we've seen people jump back onto the train within a week or two without reaping any benefit from the time off, just because they could not stand to be away from work.

Find a program

While a time-out can be little more than a refreshing pause, a leadership or executive development program is a more structured strategy, guiding people as they explore their dreams and open new doors.

Remember John Lauer? Two years after Lauer left BFGoodrich, he was still working with Hungarian refugees (his time-out) and maintained that he wanted nothing to do with running a company. Yet as part of his search for the next phase of his career, he decided to pursue an executive doctorate degree. While in the program, he took a leadership development seminar in which a series of exercises forced him to clarify his values, philosophy, aspirations, and strengths. (See the sidebar "Tools for Reflection" to learn more about some of these exercises.)

In considering the next decade of his life and reflecting on his capabilities, Lauer realized that his resistance to running a company actually represented a fear of replicating his experience at BFGoodrich. In fact, he loved being at the helm of an organization where he could convey his vision and lead the company forward, and he relished working with a team of like-minded executives. Suddenly, he realized that he missed those aspects of the CEO job and that in the right kind of situation—one in which he could apply the ideas he'd developed in his studies—being a CEO could be fun.

With this renewed passion to lead, Lauer returned a few headhunters' calls and within a month was offered the job of chairman and CEO at Oglebay Norton, a $250 million company in the raw-materials business. There he became an exemplar of the democratic leadership style, welcoming employees' input and encouraging his leadership team to do the same. As one of his executives told us, "John raises our spirits, our confidence, and our passion for excellence." Although the company deals in such unglamorous commodities as gravel and sand, Lauer made so many improvements in his first year that Oglebay Norton was featured in *Fortune*, *Business Week*, and the *Wall Street Journal*.

TOOLS FOR REFLECTION

Once you've lost touch with your passion and dreams, the very routine of work and the habits of your mind can make it difficult to reconnect. Here are some tools that can help you break from those routines and allow your dreams to resurface.

Reflecting on the Past

Alone and with trusted friends and advisers, periodically do a reality check. Take an hour or two and draw your "lifeline." Beginning with childhood, plot the high points and the low points: the events that caused you great joy and great sorrow. Note the times you were most proud, most excited, and most strong and clear. Note also the times you felt lost and alone. Point out for yourself the transitions—times when things fundamentally changed for you. Now look at the whole. What are some of the underlying themes? What seems to be ever present, no matter the situation? What values seem to weigh in most often and most heavily when you make changes in your life? Are you generally on a positive track, or have there been lots of ups and downs? Where does luck or fate fit in?

Now switch to the more recent past, and consider these questions: What has or has not changed at work and in life? How am I feeling? How do I see myself these days? Am I living my values? Am I having fun? Do my values still fit with what I need to do at work and with

(*continued*)

TOOLS FOR REFLECTION

what my company is doing? Have my dreams changed? Do I still believe in my vision of my future?

As a way to pull it all together, do a bit of free-form writing. Try finishing the sentence, "In my life I . . ." and "Now I . . ."

Defining Your Principles for Life

Think about the different aspects of your life that are important, such as family, relationships, work, spirituality, and physical health. What are your core values in each of those areas? List five or six principles that guide you in life, and think about whether they are values that you truly live by or simply talk about.

Extending the Horizon

Try writing a page or two about what you would like to do with the rest of your life. Or you might want to number a sheet of paper 1 through 27, and then list all the things you want to do or experience before you die. Don't feel the need to stop at 27, and don't worry about priorities or practicality—just write down whatever comes to you.

This exercise is harder than it seems because it's human nature to think more in terms of what we have to do—by tomorrow, next week, or next month. But with such a short horizon, we can focus only on what's urgent, not on what's important. When we think in terms of the extended horizon, such as what we might do before we die, we open up a new range of possibilities. In our work with leaders who perform this exercise, we've seen a surprising trend: Most people jot down a few career goals, but 80% or more of their lists have nothing to do with work. When they finish the exercise and study their writing, they see patterns that help them begin to crystallize their dreams and aspirations.

Envisioning the Future

Think about where you would be sitting and reading this article if it were 15 years from now and you were living your ideal life. What kinds of people would be around you? How would your environment look and feel? What might you be doing during a typical day or week? Don't worry about the feasibility of creating this life; rather, let the image develop and place yourself in the picture.

Try doing some free-form writing about this vision of yourself, speak your vision into a tape recorder, or talk about it with a trusted friend. Many people report that, when doing this exercise, they experience a release of energy and feel more optimistic than they had even moments earlier. Envisioning an ideal future can be a powerful way to connect with the possibilities for change in our lives.

Another executive we know, Tim Schramko, had a long career managing health care companies. As a diversion, he began teaching part-time. He took on a growing course load while fulfilling his business responsibilities, but he was running himself ragged. It wasn't until he went through a structured process to help him design his ideal future that he realized he had a calling to teach. Once that was clear, he developed a plan for extricating himself from his business obligations over a two-year period and is now a full-time faculty member.

Many educational institutions offer programs that support this type of move. What's more, some companies have developed their own programs because they realize that leaders who have a chance to reconnect with their dreams tend to return with redoubled energy and commitment. The risk, of course, is that after serious reflection, participants will jump ship. But in our experience, most find new meaning and passion in their current positions. In any event, people who do leave weren't in the right job—and they would have realized it sooner or later.

Create "reflective structures"

When leadership guru Warren Bennis interviewed leaders from all walks of life in the early 1990s, he found that they had a common way of staying in touch with what was important to them. They built into their lives what Bennis calls "reflective structures," time and space for self-examination, whether a few hours a week, a day or two a month, or a longer period every year.

For many people, religious practices provide an outlet for reflection, and some people build time into the day or week for prayer or meditation. But reflection does not have to involve organized religion. Exercise is an outlet for many people, and some executives set aside time in their calendars for regular workouts. One CEO of a $2 billion utility company reserves eight hours a week for solitary reflection—an hour a day, perhaps two or three hours on a weekend. During that time, he might go for a long walk, work in his home shop, or take a ride on his Harley. However you spend the time, the idea is to get away from the demands of your job and be with your own thoughts.

Increasingly, we've seen people seek opportunities for collective reflection as well, so that they can share their dreams and frustrations with their peers. On his third time heading a major division of the Hay Group, Murray Dalziel decided to build some reflection into his life by joining a CEO group that meets once a month. In a sense, the group legitimizes time spent thinking, talking, and learning from one another. Members have created a trusting community where they can share honest feedback—a scarce resource for most executives. And all gain tangible benefits, as people exchange tips on how to fix broken processes or navigate sticky situations.

Work with a coach

Our own biases and experiences sometimes make it impossible for us to find a way out of a difficult or confusing situation; we need an outside perspective. Help can come informally from family, friends, and colleagues, or it can come from a professional coach skilled at helping people see their strengths and identify new ways to use them. We won't discuss more traditional therapy in this article, but it is, of course, another alternative.

When Bob McDowell, the HR director, stepped out of his career, he sought out a variety of personal and professional connections to help him decide how to approach the future. Working with an executive coach, McDowell was able to identify what was important to him in life and translate that to what he found essential in a job. He could then draw clear lines around the aspects of his personal life he would no longer compromise, including health and exercise, time with his family, personal hobbies, and other interests. In the end, he found his way to a new career as a partner in an executive search business—a job he'd never considered but one that matched his passion for helping people and the companies they work for. What's more, his soul-searching had so sparked his creativity that in his new position he combined traditional organizational consulting with the search process to discover unusual possibilities. Instead of a typical executive search, he helps companies find employees who will bring magic to the business and to the relationships essential to success.

What did the coach bring to McDowell's self-reflection? Perhaps the chief benefit was a trusting, confidential relationship that gave him the space to dream— something executives shy away from, largely because the expectations of society and their families weigh on them so heavily. Like many, McDowell began this process assuming that he would simply narrow his priorities, clarify his work goals, and chart a new professional path. But to his surprise, his coach's perspective helped him see new opportunities in every part of his life, not just in his work.

Sometimes, however, a coach does little more than help you recognize what you already know at some level. Richard Whiteley, the cofounder of a successful international consulting firm and author of several business best-sellers, felt that he wasn't having as much fun as he used to; he was restless and wanted a change. To that end, he began to do some work on the side, helping businesspeople improve their effectiveness through spiritual development. He was considering leaving his consulting practice behind altogether and concentrating on the spiritual work—but he was torn. He turned to a spiritual leader, who told him, "Forget the spiritual work and concentrate on the work you've been doing." Only when forced to choose the wrong path could Richard recognize what he truly wanted to do. Within a few months, Richard had devoted himself to writing and speaking almost exclusively on spirituality and passion in work— and he's thriving.

Find new meaning in familiar territory

It's not always feasible to change your job or move somewhere new, even if your situation is undesirable. And frankly, many people don't want to make such major changes. But it is often easier than you might think to make small adjustments so that your work more directly reflects your beliefs and values—as long as you know what you need and have the courage to take some risks.

Back to Niall FitzGerald, who was confronted with the decision over whether to live and work in South Africa. A strong and principled person as well as a good corporate citizen, FitzGerald eventually decided to break with company culture by accepting the job on one unprecedented condition: If over the first six months or so he found his involvement with the country intolerable, he would be allowed to take another job at Unilever, no questions asked. He then set forth to find ways to exert a positive influence on his new work environment wherever possible.

As the leader of a prominent business, FitzGerald had some clout, of course, but he knew that he could not take on the government directly. His response: Figure out what he *could* change, do it, and then deal with the system. For example, when he was building a new plant, the architect showed FitzGerald plans with eight bathrooms—four each for men and women, segregated by the four primary racial groups, as mandated by law. Together, the eight bathrooms would consume one-quarter of an entire floor.

FitzGerald rejected the plans, announcing that he would build two bathrooms, one for men and one for women, to the highest possible standards. Once the plant was built, government officials inspected the building, noticed the discrepancy, and asked him what he planned to do about it. He responded, "They're not segregated because we chose not to do so. We don't agree with segregation. These are very fine toilets . . . you could have your lunch on the floor . . . . I don't have a problem at all. You have a problem, and you have to decide what you are going to do. I'm doing nothing." The government did not respond immediately, but later the law was quietly changed. FitzGerald's act of rebellion was small, but it was consistent with his values and was the only stand he could have taken in good conscience. Living one's values in this way, in the face of opposition, is energizing. Bringing about change that can make a difference to the people around us gives meaning to our work, and for many people, it leads to a renewed commitment to their jobs.

For Rob, the manager who found himself reporting to an abusive boss, the first step was to look inward and admit that every day would be a challenge. By becoming very clear about his own core values, he could decide moment to moment how to deal with Martin's demands. He could determine whether a particular emotional reaction was a visceral response to a man he didn't respect or a reaction to a bad idea that he would need to confront. He could choose whether to do what he thought was right or to collude with what felt wrong. His clarity allowed him to stay calm and focused, do his job well, and take care of the business and the people around him. In the end, Rob came out of a difficult situation knowing he had kept his integrity without compromising his career, and in that time, he even learned and grew professionally. He still uses the barometer he developed during his years with Martin to check actions and decisions against his values, even though his circumstances have changed.

Another executive we've worked with, Bart Morrison, ran a nonprofit organization for 10 years and was widely considered a success by donors, program recipients, and policy makers alike. Yet he felt restless and wondered if a turn as a company executive—which would mean higher compensation—would satisfy his urge for a new challenge. Morrison didn't really need more money, although it would have been a plus, and he had a deep sense of social mission and commitment to his work. He also acknowledged that working in the private sector would not realistically offer him any meaningful new challenges. In our work together, he brainstormed about different avenues he could take while continuing in the nonprofit field, and it occurred to him that he could write books and give speeches. These new activities gave him the excitement he had been looking for and allowed him to stay true to his calling.

It's worth noting that executives often feel threatened when employees start asking, "Am I doing what I want to do with my life?" The risk is very real that the answer will be no, and companies can lose great contributors. The impulse, then, may be to try to suppress such exploration. Many executives also avoid listening to their own signals, fearing that a close look at their dreams and aspirations will reveal severe disappointments, that to be true to themselves they will have to leave their jobs and sacrifice everything they have worked so hard to achieve.

But although people no longer expect leaders to have all the answers, they do expect their leaders to be open to the questions—to try to keep their own passion alive and to support employees through the same process. After all, sooner or later most people will feel an urgent need to take stock—and if they are given the chance to heed the call, they will most likely emerge stronger, wiser, and more determined than ever.

Richard Boyatzis is a professor in the departments of organizational behavior, psychology, and cognitive science at the Weatherhead School of Management and Distinguished University Professor at Case Western Reserve University. He is a cofounder of the Coaching Research Lab and coauthor of *Helping People Change* (Harvard Business Review Press, 2019). **Annie McKee** is a senior fellow at the University of Pennsylvania Graduate School of Education, where she teaches and leads the PennCLO Executive Doctoral Program and the MedEd Master's program. Her latest book is *How to Be Happy at Work: The Power of Purpose, Hope, and Friendship* (Harvard Business Review Press, 2017). **Daniel Goleman** is codirector of the Consortium for Research on Emotional Intelligence in Organizations at Rutgers University. His latest book is *Altered Traits: Science Reveals How Meditation Changes Your Mind, Brain, and Body* (Avery, 2017) with coauthor Richard J. Davidson. Boyatzis, McKee, and Goleman are coauthors of *Primal Leadership: Unleashing the Power of Emotional Intelligence* (Harvard Business Review Press, 2013).

Preventing Burnout on Your Team

CHAPTER 15

Making Work Less Stressful and More Engaging for Your Employees

by Natalia Peart

We all know that excessive stress is a health hazard. What is less talked about are the effects of burnout on business performance. Stress makes people nearly three times as likely to leave their jobs, temporarily impairs strategic thinking, and dulls creative abilities. Burnout, then, is a threat to your bottom line, one that costs the U.S. more than $300 billion a year in absenteeism,

Adapted from content posted on hbr.org, November 5, 2019 (product #H058FR).

turnover, diminished productivity, and medical, legal, and insurance costs.[1]

The more companies realize this, the more the workplace wellness sector grows. But individual-level perks are not the answer to our problem. In a recent study, researchers found that while there is an expectation that wellness programs will reduce health-care spending and absenteeism within a year or two, they often do not.[2] This study adds to the growing body of work suggesting that such programs are not as effective as we think.

Instead, employers need to shift to organization-level approaches for reducing stress at work, ones that foster employee well-being while simultaneously improving business performance. While this may seem unrealistic, it's not. Over a decade of experience as a clinical psychologist and leadership consultant has taught me that burnout prevention requires reducing workplace stress while also upping employee engagement. Here's how to do both.

Create a Work Environment That Decreases Stress

When employees are put in a high-stress situation—whether from unclear expectations, unreasonable deadlines, or a hectic workspace—they are at risk of moving into fight-or-flight mode. This is something that happens to our bodies when we feel threatened. The primal, more emotional parts of our brains take over, and our ability to think long term, strategize, and innovate decreases. If we stay in this mode too long, eventually, we get burned out. To counter this effect, you need to build a secure work environment and incorporate stress reduction habits into your team's daily workflows.

Increase psychological safety

If your employees perceive your workplace as a threat, then you cannot build the trust your team needs to collaborate and innovate effectively. In her book *The Fearless Organization*, Amy Edmondson describes three steps you can take to build psychological safety. First, make your expectations obvious by giving your employees clear goals. Second, make sure everyone feels that their voices are heard, and that everyone knows that you *want* their voices to be heard. You can do this by inviting people to speak up in meetings and conducting brainstorming sessions more than you impose top-down decisions. Third, develop a work environment that is both challenging and unthreatening. Let people know it's OK to fail. Recognize team members who think outside the box and ask your employees for feedback regularly to show you're all in it together.

Build regular break times into the workday

The human brain can focus for around 90–120 minutes before it needs to rest. That's why you should encourage your employees to step away from their desks and mentally disengage from challenging tasks every couple of hours. Suggest they go for a short walk (especially if they have been in a series of long meetings), send out calendar invites reminding them to take breaks, and try to lead by example. Letting their minds rest and moving their bodies will provide your team with the mental space they need to perform well consistently.

Encourage the use of private workspaces when team members need to focus

Open offices are prone to distractions, increasing stress and decreasing productivity. There is sometimes a built-in expectation that employees must always be available for impromptu meetings and discussions as a result of the office layout. If you don't have private workspaces where employees can go to focus or decompress, try using signals like "do not disturb" signs when needed, or scheduling "quiet hours" when people can work.

Set boundaries around time outside of work

Teams that are not all in one location might need to work outside of traditional hours from time to time. However, the blurring of work and personal time is a significant source of job stress. A study found that it is not just answering emails that increases employees' anxiety—it is also the expectation that they will be available to do so outside of work hours. To combat this, set clear guidelines and follow them. Send emails and make calls after hours only when it's urgent—and set the bar very high.

Look into flexible work policies

If you want a highly adaptive team, then create an adaptable work environment. Give your employees flexibility by allowing them to work staggered hours, taking into account their varying needs. Hold one-on-one meetings to understand those needs and find alternative arrangements for people who are struggling with work-life balance.

Build Employee Engagement

Decades of data have confirmed that higher employee engagement, or the strength of the mental and emotional connection an employee feels toward their workplace, has many positive benefits—including reduced stress, improved health and job satisfaction, as well as increased productivity, job retention, and profitability.

Be transparent

If your team members are confused about how their work connects to and serves both the short- and long-term company goals, they will naturally become more stressed and less productive—especially in times of uncertainty. Part of your job is to help them see the big picture, or the role they play in helping the company achieve its larger goals. While you may not be able to share everything with your team, you can provide them with the information they need to understand how their work is contributing to the company's mission. If they are curious about something that you are unable to share, be transparent about why. You want to reduce the stress that accompanies ambiguity. One study of 2.5 million teams found that, when managers communicated daily with their direct reports, employees were three times as likely to be engaged than when their managers did not communicate regularly with them.[3] Still, only

40% of employees say they are well informed about their company's strategic goals.

Make sure people are in the right roles

If your team members loathe doing their jobs, then they are naturally going to be less engaged. To ensure that their talents and strengths are aligned with the expectations and responsibilities of their roles, check in with each of your direct reports regularly. These conversations don't need to be formal—talk to them about their passions, interests, and goals. Use the information you gather to assign projects they will find meaningful and follow up to ensure they have the tools they need to succeed.

Give as much autonomy as you can

When possible, give your team control over how they manage their projects. Employees are 43% less likely to experience high levels of burnout when they have a choice in deciding what tasks to do, when to do them, and how much time to spend on each.[4] To make sure someone is ready to work independently, one researcher suggests asking them to shadow you on a task or project first, and then allowing them to practice under your supervision. During this time, you can give them feedback and gauge when they will be ready to work on their own.

Demonstrate a commitment to your employees' growth and progression

Don't hold on too tightly to your talent. While most people will not be promoted every year or two, they do need to feel like you are providing them with steady growth and learning opportunities. Sometimes this might even mean supporting internal mobility. Give people the chance to move around, or move on, if it's the right next step for their careers. Your commitment to their growth will deepen the sense of trust between you and them.

Create a culture of recognition

Publicly recognizing the hard work and contributions of team members decreases feelings of stress and increases feelings of connection and belonging. Research has shown that companies with high-recognition cultures perform better and have less turnover than those that don't. This is, perhaps, because support and recognition make it easier for people to cope with the demands of work by showing them that their efforts are valued. Team meetings are a great time to call out exceptional performance. Unexpected gestures that communicate sincere appreciation can also be effective. If your employee closes a new client deal, for example, congratulate them publicly. Josh Bersin of Deloitte adds that if you can create a culture in which peers recognize and show gratitude to one another, your employees are more likely to stay happy and satisfied in their roles.[5]

Deepen engagement further by instilling a sense of purpose

If the only thing motivating your team to go to work is a paycheck, their performance will suffer more than those who feel a sense of purpose in what they do. When employees connect the impact of their work back to the real world, daily tasks, which once seemed tedious, gain meaning. Start by making purpose a part of your business plan. Even if it's not declared in your mission statement, help your team understand by showing them the impact their work has both within the company, in other departments, as well as outside the organization, on society. You should also share your purpose during recruitment, and search for candidates that support it.

Burnout and the consequences it reaps when unacknowledged are detrimental to employee well-being and business performance. To battle this growing epidemic and create healthier work environments, leaders need to commit to changing what "workplace wellness" looks like. Let these steps guide you. If you are successful, you will not just reduce worker stress. You will create a workforce with happier, more productive employees, and be a better business for it.

Natalia Peart, PhD, is a clinical psychologist and *Fortune* 1000 executive leadership consultant. She has served on the Federal Reserve Board, 10th District; as staff psychologist at Johns Hopkins University; and CEO of the Women's Center for Advancement. She is also the author of *Future Proofed: How to Navigate Disruptive Change, Find Calm in Chaos, and Succeed in Work & Life.*

NOTES

1. American Institute of Stress, "Are You Experiencing Workplace Stress?," survey, n.d., https://www.stress.org/workplace-stress.

2. Zirui Song and Katherine Baicker, "Effect of Workplace Wellness Program on Employee Health and Economic Outcomes," *JAMA* 321, no. 15 (2019): 1491–1501.

3. "State of the American Manager," Gallup, n.d., https://www.gallup.com/services/182138/state-american-manager.aspx.

4. Ryan Pendell, "Millennials Are Burning Out," Gallup, July 19, 2018, https://www.gallup.com/workplace/237377/millennials-burning.aspx.

5. Josh Bersin, "Becoming Irresistible: A New Model for Employee Engagement," Deloitte Insights, January 27, 2015, https://www2.deloitte.com/us/en/insights/deloitte-review/issue-16/employee-engagement-strategies.html#endnote-sup-37.

CHAPTER 16

How Are You Protecting Your High Performers?

by Matt Plummer

A little over a year ago, a high-performing specialist at one of the largest technologies companies—we'll call him Santiago—was given an opportunity no high performer could turn down: an opportunity to play a manager role on a project he really cared about. The director told him, "You care about this; you lead it." So he did, and all seemed to be going well—even though he was planning a significant companywide event at the same time, a role he had volunteered for.

Adapted from "How Are You Protecting Your High Performers from Burnout?" on hbr.org, June 21, 2018 (product #H04ETX).

"We had a really important conference call I had spent a lot of time preparing for. The call went well, but when I finished the call, I realized I was feeling really sick," Santiago recounts. "It got worse after that. I went to the doctor later that day, and he told me I had pneumonia. I ended up in the ER the next morning and couldn't work for the full next week. It was a shocking moment for me. I'm young and healthy, but I realized that if I push myself, I will burn out."

Unfortunately, this isn't an unusual experience for high performers: A five-year study in the U.K. found that the mental health of 20% of the top-performing leaders of U.K. businesses is affected by corporate burnout.[1]

It's easy to blame burnout on the high performers themselves. After all, the stereotype is that these over-achievers say yes to more work even when they're already at capacity. They routinely put work first, canceling personal engagements to finish the job.

While such habits may be partially to blame, this isn't the full story. In my experience, many companies and leaders engage in three common practices, often unknowingly, that make top performers even more likely to burn out:

They Put High Performers on the Hardest Projects

"The most obvious difference between high performers and their peers is that high performers are put on the hardest projects over and over again. There are no 'softball' projects," says a high-performing manager at a leading strategy and management consulting firm, who we'll call Lisa. It makes sense: Of course, you'd want your best people on the most important projects. But if you keep going back to the same small group of people time and time again, you'll run the risk of wearing them out.

They Use High Performers to Compensate for Weaker Team Members

Lisa describes another unique characteristic of the experience of high performers: "You're seen as an exemplary employee, so you're expected to support lower performers and mentor others." A senior manager from a leading technology company, who we'll call Karen, recounts her experience on a project where this was true: "I spent a lot of time trying to coach and mentor them and quite honestly taking on a lot of their work because you feel that is what you're supposed to do when others are struggling." While many star performers do enjoy mentoring others, they understandably start to feel resentful if they think the boss is letting poor performers off the hook.

They Ask High Performers to Help on Many Small Efforts Unrelated to Their Work

"As a high performer, you have demands as a culture carrier, a mentor, and a resource for others," Lisa says. Similarly, Karen describes how this practice affects her and her high-performing team members: "They are constantly being asked to help in small ways. 'You're good at making slides. Can you make this one slide?' 'You're good at WordPress. Can you add this page?' I'm just realizing how much time I've spent on all these one-off requests the last few weeks. And that's why I don't feel like I've gotten anything done." While this issue is often framed as a personal problem for people who don't know how to set boundaries or say no, it's more fairly seen as an organizational problem where the most hardworking people are "rewarded" with more work.

To fix this, managers can start by becoming more aware of how these practices are affecting their organizations and looking to scale them back when possible. Beyond that, employers and leaders should look to three other strategies to help them support their high performers for the long term.

Let High Performers Occasionally Pick Their Projects

High performers generally are very motivated by the work. Yet, they don't regularly get the option to do the projects they care most about unless it happens to also be the hardest project available, or unless they agree to do it on top of their normal work. Letting them choose some of their projects reconnects them with the reason they are excited to do their job—something that can get lost in the throes of burnout.

Lisa explains how such an opportunity saved her consulting job: "When I asked to be on a new project, I was managing a big team in addition to my other work, which included an exceptionally busy project. On the team I was managing, there was a low performer who was put on the team specifically for me to mentor and an inexperienced team member who couldn't work too independently . . . To add to all that, the partner was largely unavailable. I basically had to carry the team. After all that, I probably would have left if they hadn't granted my request to go on the project I asked for."

Create High-Performing Pairs

High performers routinely find themselves separated from those they most closely relate to and enjoy working with. This happens for obvious reasons, but surrounding them with low performers increases their workload, saps their morale, and limits their development. Pairing two high performers of *a similar level* can help distribute this added weight and improve high performers' experience without leaving some teams with no high performers. "When I got to work with other high performers, it felt like a totally different experience. Not only did it make me feel more motivated, but it made me better because the other high performers were pushing my thinking. That's how you keep high performers growing. It's not just putting them on the hardest projects," Lisa says.

It's important to emphasize that these pairs should consist of employees at the same or a similar level. Placing a high-performing entry-level employee with a high-performing leader won't have the same effect.

Keep Track of Additional Demands on Their Time

Demands unrelated to core work are unsuspected drivers of burnout because they each feel so insignificant and it's hard to keep track of their aggregate effect. Karen offers the transition she put her team through as an example of how to address this: "We get a lot of requests into our team, and because we all want to serve others and say yes, we ended up spending all our time on work not related to our priorities. I spent a few months breaking them of that by saying, 'You don't have the authority to say yes to anything. You can't say yes or no. You need to talk to me. It's my job to balance all priorities.' And this gives them a layer of protection."

Employers or leaders won't always need to be as draconian as this. In many cases, simply keeping track of all the requests in a single place can equip high performers with the awareness to turn down some of the incoming requests.

These three strategies may seem to offer only marginal benefits, but it's the accumulation of small savings and improvements that reduces the risk of burnout over time. High performers hold great value for any company, delivering 400% more productivity than average performers. Companies will lose much of this value if they don't take deliberate action to protect their high performers from burnout.

Matt Plummer is the founder of Zarvana, which offers online programs and coaching services to help working professionals become more productive by developing time-saving habits. Before starting Zarvana, Matt spent six years at Bain & Company spinout The Bridgespan Group, a strategy and management consulting firm for nonprofits, foundations, and philanthropists. Follow him on Twitter @mtplummer.

NOTE

1. Diane Wood, "Corporate Burnout Affecting the Mental Health of 20 Percent of Top Performers in UK Businesses," *Personnel Today*, May 3, 2017.

CHAPTER 17

How to Help Your Team with Burnout When You're Burned Out Yourself

by Rebecca Knight

As a manager, you want to do right by your employees and support them through intense work periods so they don't get burned out. But this can be a challenge when you're feeling overly stressed yourself. How can you take care of yourself so that you have the time and energy to

Adapted from content posted on hbr.org, March 20, 2019 (reprint #H04URE).

support your team? What steps do you need to take to reduce your stress level? And what actions can you take to improve your team members' well-being?

What the Experts Say

It's tough to find the energy you need to help others when you yourself are at your limits. Burnout—as opposed to more run-of-the-mill stress—can cause you to "feel utterly depleted," says Susan David, a founder of the Harvard/McLean Institute of Coaching and author of *Emotional Agility*. And it "can permeate all aspects of your life. You are overtired and underexercised; you're not attentive to food and nutrition; and you're disconnected from relationships." But it's not just you who suffers. "Your team is picking up on your stress, and it's making everything worse," says Whitney Johnson, the author of *Disrupt Yourself*. So for the sake of both your health and the health of your employees, you need to summon all the resources you can to improve matters. Here's how to do that.

Make your own health a priority

Before you can help your team members manage their stress, you need to manage your own. "Instead of hunkering down and concentrating" on your job, "you need to stop, look around, and figure out how you're going to help your people get what they need," says Johnson. A good starting point is to take care of your physical and mental health. Eat healthy, wholesome food; exercise regularly; get plenty of sleep at night; "try meditating and find someone to vent to"—preferably "not your boss." Taking care of yourself is not an indulgent luxury; it's a matter of self-preservation. Johnson suggests sharing your tension-management techniques and rituals with your team. "Say, 'Here's something I'm doing to manage the stress. This is how I cope.'"

Tackle the problem as a group

Even if you haven't fully reined in your stress, it's helpful to demonstrate that you take the issue seriously. You can even suggest that you all take on self-care as a team—learning meditation as a group or sharing tips about what practices are working to reduce stress. You can make it a team goal to keep stress under control, says David. "Say to your team, 'Even in the context of this change, how do we come together?'" This is helpful for the group but will also keep you accountable for taking care of yourself. Don't force anyone into these activities though. A sense of autonomy can counteract the symptoms of burnout, so you want people to feel they are making their own choices.

Exhibit compassion

Don't be so hard on yourself or your team. "Burnout can often feel like a personal failing," says David. But of course, that's not true: We are all susceptible to it—and, in fact, our "environment precipitates" it. We are "living in an imperfect world, and yet we expect perfection." Many organizations breed stress. "The ambiguity, the complexity," not to mention the 24/7 nature of technology, leads many of us to feel "an extreme level of strain." Be compassionate. Recognize, both inwardly and publicly, "that all of us are doing the best we can with the resources we have been given." This doesn't mean that you're "lazy or letting yourself off the hook." Rather, you're "creating a psychologically safe place for yourself and others." Johnson recommends talking your team through stressful periods in an honest but upbeat way. Yes, the workload is intense. And yes, big, high-stakes projects are daunting. Tell your team, "We are in this together, and I know we can deliver."

Set a good example

You also need to "think about the [behaviors] you're modeling" to your team, says David. "If you're running from meeting to meeting and don't have enough time in the day to breathe," what message does that send? Set a good example by making downtime a priority. Show your team that you don't always operate in full-throttle mode at the office. "Bring humanity back into the room," she says. Johnson agrees. When "your people are completely overwhelmed," you need to "encourage them to take regular breaks," she says. "They need time to rest and rejuvenate and disconnect from work." It's also important to set limits on how much work encroaches on evenings and weekends. Whatever you do, "don't send anyone on your team an email at midnight," says Johnson. "You're thinking, 'I've got to get this out.' But you're also throwing a grenade into your employees' peace of mind." Instead, she recommends using Boomerang, or a similar program, that allows you to schedule emails.

Focus on the why

A common symptom (and cause) of job-related burnout is a "disconnect between a person's values" and the work at hand, says David. "You feel stressed and tired, and yet you continue to work and work and work," all the while forgetting what drew you to your career and organization in the first place. "It can be toxic." As a leader, you need to "develop a shared sense of why"—as in, why are we driven to accomplish the mission? As a boss, it's your job to galvanize your team. Remind them of the objective and why it's important to the organization and your customers. When people have shared values and connection, they are more likely to feel positively about their work.

Advocate for your team

If you and your team are suffering under a heavy workload, it might be time to ask your boss for a reprieve. It is your responsibility "to advocate for your team within the context of your organization's goals," says Johnson. She recommends talking to your boss about the effect stress is having on morale and performance. "Say, 'My team is fully committed to this project, but people are tired. And we all know the law of diminishing returns.'" Convey the consequences of burnout and describe how it is in your boss's best interest to take action. "There are going to be mistakes and slippage. And those will be costly." Explain that you're worried you might lose people who are valuable to the organization. Then ask, "Can this deadline be pushed back? Or can this assignment be curtailed?"

Think, too, about what you can "put in place within your team that can help," says David. Perhaps certain meetings can be discarded or at least shortened. It's "important that leaders go to bat" for their employees.

Be a source of optimism

Whenever work is frenzied and frantic, make a concerted effort to promote positivity, says Johnson. This is hard to do when you are stressed out, but "look for the good," she says. "Smile at people. And be kind." Make sure you regularly acknowledge, recognize, and thank people for their efforts. "Say, 'I notice you did X. Thank you. I appreciate it.'" Cultivate a feeling of community and social support. When your team hits a milestone or when a particular crunch time is over, celebrate. Acknowledge the accomplishments—yours and the team's.

Rebecca Knight is a freelance journalist in Boston and a lecturer at Wesleyan University. Her work has been published in the *New York Times*, *USA Today*, and the *Financial Times*.

CHAPTER 18

Three Ways to Break Your Employees Out of the Busyness Paradox

by Brigid Schulte

For most of my working life, I've felt way too busy. Sometimes heart-stoppingly, wildly so—working long hours, missing out on family time or fun, and stressed beyond belief. And yet, a few years ago, as I was cleaning out my file cabinet before leaving the *Washington Post*

Adapted from "Preventing Busyness from Becoming Burnout," on hbr.org, April 15, 2019 (product #H04W6D).

after nearly 20 years, I found folder after folder of half-reported stories that would have been good. Really good. If only I hadn't been too busy to actually work on them.

In the years since, I've thought about that moment with a mix of shame and regret. I largely blamed myself for not making the time to do more ambitious, high-priority work, or managing to get it all done within reasonable hours and have more time for life. It's only recently that I've begun to see how I was trapped in a busyness tunnel.

During the past two and a half years, I've been working on a project with researchers from ideas42 (a non-profit that uses behavioral science to solve real-world problems) to explore whether behavioral science design can help solve issues of work-life conflict. Our research finds that this conflict—which is a potent cause of stress and a key contributor to increases in poor health, a drop-off in productivity, and the stall in gender equality—is largely the result of how workers experience busyness.

And perhaps most importantly, we've concluded that ending the busyness cycle may not be something workers can do on their own. The most promising solutions are at the organizational, not the personal, level.

How Workers Experience Work-Life Conflict

It's taken some time to get to these insights. In the first phase of the project, researchers with ideas42 spent about a year working with three different nonprofit philanthropic organizations around the country. They made a couple of site visits to interview and observe the work styles of workers, managers, and leaders; the work culture; and how people interacted with their work environment to better understand the factors that drive work-life conflict. In the current phase, ideas42 scoped out five other nonprofit organizations and are working with three that have committed to design and test specific behavioral interventions to try to reduce it.

As we reviewed some of the most recent site work, I was struck by one powerful disconnect that came up over and over again: At virtually every organization, everyone interviewed said that work-life balance—the ability to work effectively and have time for a fulfilling and healthy life outside of work—is a core value of the organization. And yet, every organization (including ideas42 and the Better Life Lab, the nonprofit program I now direct) struggles to live that value. Emails can fly at all hours. Work spills into nights, weekends, vacations, hospital waiting rooms, and family celebrations. People are feeling burned out. And yet despite this, many workers very publicly wear this overworked, overly busy work martyrdom like a badge of honor. At one organization, workers said they felt that no one should work more than 45 hours a week. Yet the typical employee actually works more than 52.

Mission-driven nonprofits face a particular challenge. Workers there often think that their work is so important that it matters more than their compensation, health, or work-life balance. In fact, one recent study found that as many as half of all nonprofit employees are either burned out or on the verge of it. On the site visits, some workers said that, while they saw the benefit of work-life balance, they worked to the point of exhaustion because they love what they do. "We think [our work is] important, so it creates a disincentive in some ways to turn it off," one participant told us. "If we all hated our jobs, it would be much easier to create work-life balance."

Leaders didn't fare much better. While they expressed a desire for better work-life balance—if not for themselves, at least for the rest of their staff—they were often among the worst offenders, texting at 9 p.m., emailing over the weekend or at night, and rarely taking vacation. Some leaders weren't even aware how what they did (overwork) undermined what they said they believed (that work-life balance is important). Other leaders knew they weren't walking the talk: "We do a poor job modeling work-life balance," said one.

I realized then that really creating better work-life effectiveness would require more than just telling people to log out of email at night. Everyone at these work sites knew what they *should be doing*, but *actually doing it* was a different story. So whatever behavioral interventions researchers designed would have to address workplace cultures trapped in a broader busyness paradox.

The Busyness Paradox, Explained

Here's how the busyness paradox works: When we're busy and have that high-octane, panicked feeling that time is scarce—what one participant called the "sustained moment of hecticness" through the workday—our attention and ability to focus narrow. Behavioral researchers call this phenomenon "tunneling." And, like being in a tunnel, we're only able to concentrate on the most immediate, and often low value, tasks right in front of us. (Research has found we actually lose about 13 IQ points in this state.) We run around putting out fires all day, racing to meetings, plowing through emails, and getting to 5 or 6 p.m. with the sick realization that we haven't even started our most important work of the day.

So we stay late at the office, or take work home in the evenings or weekends, and effectively steal time for work away from the rest of our lives. "If you're in this firefighting state of time pressure and tunneling, you're not making time to meet long-term goals. You're not dealing with any of the root causes that led to the firefighting in the first place," said Matthew Darling, ideas42 vice president and project lead. "The tendency is to do the stuff that's easy to check off. That's all you have the bandwidth for." Tunneling and busyness are mutually reinforcing, Darling added. "Focusing on short-term tasks makes you not make strategic plans, which causes you to be busy."

In theory, workers could just ignore any work they didn't complete before, say, 5 p.m., and call it a day. But it's hard to break out of the tunnel now: Unlike a century ago, when Americans showed their status in leisure time, busyness has become the new badge of honor. So even as we bemoan workplaces where everyone is busy and no one is productive, busyness has actually become the way to signal dedication to the job and leadership potential. One reason for this is that, while productivity is relatively easy to measure on a factory floor, or on the farm, we have yet to develop good metrics for measuring the productivity of knowledge workers. So we largely rely on hours worked and face time in the office as markers for effort, and with the advent of technology and the ability to work remotely, being connected and responsive at all hours is the new face time. "Tunneling is no longer something that happens by accident," Darling explained. "It's a condition that workers are forced into by standard management practices."

So how can behavioral science interventions begin to nudge this powerful busyness bias that keeps us all so stressed out?

One key will be to construct new mental models of the ideal worker. Right now, the model is someone who comes in early, eats lunch at their desk, stays late, emails at all hours, is always busy, and is always available to put work first—a definition that excludes anyone with caregiving responsibilities (who are, in the U.S., primarily women) or the desire for a healthy work-life balance.

So the interventions ideas42 is designing to improve work effectiveness and work-life balance may also wind up nudging the idea that an ideal worker in the 21st century is someone who does great work, is well rested and healthy, and has a great life outside of work—not someone who's trapped in the busy tunnel, chasing their tail, thinking small, and on the road to burn out. These interventions are designed with the very foundation of behavioral science in mind: that human decision making is shaped not by individual personality or willpower, but by the environment.

Three Ways to Break Your Employees Out of the Busyness Paradox

Recognize the power of social signals

When we're at work, all we see are other people working. And when we see late-night emails or texts, we assume that our coworker or boss has been working all day or night without interruption, when perhaps they'd been out walking the dog or having dinner with their families. But that life outside work doesn't register because we don't see it. (We often don't want to share our lives outside work with coworkers and bosses in order to preserve the busyness myth that we *are* always working.)

"You end up miscalibrating," Darling explained, or thinking that people are working more than they actually are, so you automatically think you have to as well in order to keep up. Researchers point to a classic study of such "norm misperception" and how prevalent and damaging it can be: One nationwide survey found that a large share of college students overestimated the amount of alcohol their peers consumed. Over time, the best predictor for how much students wound up drinking was how much they *thought* their peers were drinking, even though, in reality, their peers weren't drinking that much.

To correct that "always on" misperception, researchers at ideas42 are testing the idea of making non-work time more visible. They're asking managers to be more open about taking lunch breaks, leaving the office on time, working flexibly, going on vacation, talking about life outside of work or care responsibilities, and more demonstrably encouraging others to do the same—potentially even including life events on shared calendars. Another experiment involves automatic reminders. These reminders would go out at the beginning of every year and would prompt people to schedule their vacations.

Researchers are also working with teams to design email, phone, and texting protocols to cut down or eliminate work communication outside of normal hours, particularly from leaders who set expectations for everyone else. Behavior might be tracked and made transparent so that, through the powerful nudge of social comparison, people and leaders would be held accountable and the new systems more likely to stick.

Build in slack for important work

Humans are terrible at estimating how much time and effort are actually needed to accomplish things. It's called the planning fallacy, and the busyness paradox only exacerbates that tendency to underestimate and overpromise. So one intervention being tested is for workers to intentionally create slack in their calendars every week—in other words, intentionally schedule a block of slack time to finish up any work that got delayed after an emergency popped up, or to finish a project that took longer than you thought it would. The team at ideas42 came up with the idea based on a study of hospital operating rooms that found leaving one room unused for emergencies, rather than booking to 100% capacity, actually increased the number of surgical cases and revenue while cutting down on staff overwork.

Another idea is to create "transition days" at work before and after vacations, when the only expectation of workers would be to wrap up work before leaving and catch up on what they missed while they were out. That would give workers a better chance of truly unplugging and recharging during vacation, and help people ease back into work after. People won't feel as compelled to answer emails throughout for fear of falling behind, or dread juggling the awaiting inbox with immediate work demands. "You almost always need a lot more slack than you think you will," Darling explained, "and it is actually markedly important for doing good work."

Slack time requires a new mental model—recognizing that, no matter how carefully we plan, work emergencies and unexpected demands will always crop up and projects and tasks will usually require more time than we've allocated. So creating blank space isn't slacking off (pun intended); it's time that enables you to get your most important work done effectively and keeping it from spilling over into the rest of your life.

Increase transparency into everyone's workload

Many people participating in our project felt they were always busy—going to meetings, answering emails, collaborating with others—but not necessarily productive. They found it difficult to find chunks of uninterrupted time to concentrate on a big project, much less plan or think or strategize. Some even said they used their paid time off just to have a day of uninterrupted, independent work.

So one intervention that ideas42 researchers are experimenting with is an effort to "concretize" work by actually scheduling in time to work on the week's priorities and making actual workloads transparent to bosses and coworkers. The thinking is that that transparency is likely to create positive friction every time someone wants to call a meeting. With priority work made more transparent, calling a meeting won't be seen as cost free, but a values trade-off: What is everyone *not* doing because they're at this meeting? And is the meeting the better use of everyone's time?

Another idea involves "meeting hygiene"—can meetings become more efficient with a required agenda, limited time, and concrete action plan? Researchers may also test meeting and email blackout days to encourage concentrated work time.

In the end, the hope is that these interventions will help people begin to act their way into a new way of thinking. If they see they can work more effectively *and* have a healthier work-life balance, perhaps instead of praising people who brag about being super busy and working all the time, they'll begin to think: If workers aren't getting their most important work done, are on the verge of burnout, and have little time for life, what needs to change at this organization?

———————

Brigid Schulte is a journalist, author of the *New York Times* bestselling *Overwhelmed: Work, Love, and Play When No One Has the Time*, and director of the Better Life Lab at New America.

CHAPTER 19

Helping Remote Workers Avoid Loneliness and Burnout

by Jennifer Moss

As more workers work flexibly or remotely, companies need to change the way they operate. "It forces structural and systemic change to accommodate different ways of working and different ways of being 'available' and productive," Dorothy Hisgrove, a partner and chief people officer at PwC Australia, told me. Remote and flex work also present new challenges for managers.

Adapted from content posted on hbr.org, November 30, 2018 (product #H04O9G).

In particular, I call your attention to two: helping your people avoid burnout and loneliness.

Burnout

People who use flex or remote policies often feel more grateful to their employers than those who do not. That feeling of indebtedness can lead some remote employees to keep their foot on the gas until they run out of fuel. In their paper "Doing More with Less? Flexible Working Practices and the Intensification of Work," Clare Kelliher and Deirdre Anderson examine this unanticipated consequence of adopting flexible working practices. Using social exchange theory, the researchers suggest, "employees respond to the ability to work flexibly by exerting additional effort, in order to return benefit to their employer." Some of the intensification happens at the employee level (choices they make to return the favor), but frequently, it's the employer intensifying the workload with requests that can't be accomplished within certain time frames.

To ensure employees experience gratitude rather than indebted servitude, check in. Go beyond project updates and work-related conversations. Leaders need to know what is going on with their people beyond just their work. For example, be sensitive to employees who have been working heads down on a project for longer than normal. Rather than booking them into scores of virtual meetings immediately after coming up for air, give them some time to reconnect with family and recharge.

Rethink which attributes constitute going above and beyond. Working longer hours, answering emails late at night, putting time in on the weekend, working while sick, piling up vacation days, not sleeping—those attributes are way too often considered high-performing traits. However, all it does is increase and reward the behaviors of burnout. Instead, lead by example and encourage your virtual staff to slow down (even when they don't want to) by supporting mental health breaks, taking vacations, and spending time with family. As leaders, we need to set up the margins—the space to recuperate—because our virtual staff won't. Instead, when time is available, remote employees will fill in the margins with additional work.

Remember, our virtual workers are tougher to diagnose with burnout because you can't see changes in their personality on a day-to-day basis. Ensure there is a process of checking in and being aware of the signs.

Loneliness

According to the 2018 State of Remote Work, loneliness is the biggest struggle to working remotely. Although being alone is not the only cause of loneliness, it can be a significant contributor. It's also a dangerous and growing epidemic that scientists are taking seriously. We must be even more vigilant to this threat after more companies have switched to a digital-first policy.

At the 125th Annual Convention of the American Psychological Association, Dr. Julianne Holt-Lunstad from Brigham Young University presented the results of 148 studies with a total of 308,849 participants. The study laid out the connection between loneliness and premature mortality. "There is robust evidence that social isolation and loneliness significantly increase risk for premature mortality, and the magnitude of the risk exceeds that of many leading health indicators," Holt-Lunstad shared.

What can managers do? One option, when available, would be to establish an "in the office" day, when remote employees are encouraged to come in. According to a Gallup poll of 9,917 employed U.S. adults, remote workers that come in to work at least once per week are the happiest. These "mostly" remote workers report a slightly higher rate of engagement, but more importantly, they were more likely than full-remote or full-office workers to say they had a best friend at work, and that their job included opportunities to learn and grow.

For further-flung members of the team who can't come in weekly, make the investment to bring them to the office monthly or quarterly. Joe Granato, the chief supply chain officer at Mountain Equipment Co-op, told me that he believes finding the budget to gather in person should be mandatory: "Face-to-face time builds quality relationships, thus enabling trust and speed in communications. Having opportunities to be together (in the same space, not virtually) is a quality investment." Granato also advocates for a "working remotely code" to help set shared expectations and make everyone feel looped into the strategy.

Today's flexible and remote work arrangements are far more fluid than the rigid flex-plan policies of yester-year. Regardless of what HR policies may dictate, managers are going to do whatever to keep their people. That likely includes more flexible work options, paired with a management style that helps remote workers flourish.

———————

Jennifer Moss is an award-winning journalist, author, and international public speaker. She is a CBC Radio Columnist, reporting on topics related to happiness and well-being. She contributes regularly to *Harvard Business Review* and writes for the Society of Human Resource Management (SHRM). She sits on the Global Happiness Council in support of the UN's Sustainable Development Goals related to well-being. Her book *Unlocking Happiness at Work* was named Business Book of the Year and her forthcoming book on burnout will be published by Harvard Business Review Press.

How Organizations Can Combat Burnout

CHAPTER 20

Burnout Is About Your Workplace, Not Your People

by Jennifer Moss

We tend to think of burnout as an individual problem, solvable by learning to say no, more yoga, better breathing techniques, practicing resilience—the self-help list goes on. But evidence is mounting that applying personal, Band-Aid solutions to an epic and rapidly evolving workplace phenomenon may be harming, not helping, the battle. With "burnout" now officially recognized by the World Health Organization (WHO), the responsibility for managing it has shifted away from the individual

---

Adapted from content posted on hbr.org, December 11, 2019 (product #H05BI7).

and toward the organization. Leaders take note: It's now on *you* to build a burnout strategy.

It's Not Me, It's You

According to the foremost expert on burnout, Christina Maslach, social psychologist and professor emerita of psychology at the University of California, Berkeley, we are attacking the problem from the wrong angle (see chapter 24 of this guide). Maslach worries about misuses of the new WHO classification. "Categorizing burnout as a disease was an attempt by the WHO to provide definitions for what is wrong with people, instead of what is wrong with companies," she explains. "When we just look at the person, what that means is, 'Hey, we've got to treat that person.' 'You can't work here because you're the problem.' 'We have to get rid of that person.' Then, it becomes that person's problem, not the responsibility of the organization that employs them."

To Maslach's point, a survey of 7,500 full-time employees by Gallup found the top five reasons for burnout are:

1. Unfair treatment at work

2. Unmanageable workload

3. Lack of role clarity

4. Lack of communication and support from their manager

5. Unreasonable time pressure[1]

The list above clearly demonstrates that the root causes of burnout do not really lie with the individual and that they can be averted, if only leadership started prevention strategies much further upstream.

In our interview, Maslach asked me to picture a canary in a coal mine. They are healthy birds, singing away as they make their way into the cave. But, when they come out full of soot and disease, no longer singing, can you imagine us asking why the canaries made themselves sick? No, because the answer would be obvious: The *coal mine* is making the birds sick.

This visual struck me. Although developing emotional intelligence skills—like optimism, gratitude, and hope—can give people the rocket fuel they need to be successful, if an employee is dealing with burnout, we have to stop and ask ourselves why. We should never suggest that if they'd just practiced more grit or joined another yoga class or taken a mindfulness course, their burnout would have been avoided. I have long been a proponent of empathy and optimism in leadership. I believe in practicing gratitude skills for a happier, higher-performing work and life experience. I endorse the idea of building resilience to better handle stress when it arises. But these skills are not the cure for burnout, nor are they the vaccine.

So, what is?

First, ask yourself as a leader, what is making my staff so unhealthy? Why does our work environment lack the conditions for them to flourish? How can I make it safe for them to work here every day? We have to dig into the data and ask our people what would make work better for them. More generally, we need to better understand what causes people to feel motivated in our organizations, and what causes them frustration.

Motivation-Hygiene Theory

Frederick Herzberg is known for his dual-factor, motivation-hygiene theory—essentially, what motivates us versus what basic needs must be met in order to maintain job satisfaction. Herzberg found that satisfaction and dissatisfaction are not on a continuum, with one increasing as the other diminishes, but are instead independent of each other. This means that managers need to recognize and attend to both equally.

Motivators are different than hygiene factors. Motivation factors include challenging work, recognition for one's achievements, responsibility, the opportunity to do something meaningful, involvement in decision making, and a sense of importance to the organization. On the other hand, hygiene factors include salary, work conditions, company policy and administration, supervision, working relationships, and status and security.

Often, employees don't recognize when an organization has good hygiene, but bad hygiene can cause a major distraction. The latter can come down to seemingly innocuous issues, like having coffee in the break room one day and no more coffee the next. People feel it. Burnout happens when these presupposed features in our day-to-day work lives are missing or taken away.

Maslach has affectionately named this feeling "pebbles." She describes them as the tiny, incremental, irritating, and painful stuff at work that can wear you down. Through my work, I've seen this in action. Consider this example: The music faculty chairs at a university where I worked decided to put their entire annual improvement budget toward building a soundproof studio. They were certain the rest of the group would be thrilled. They were wrong. In reality, staff just wanted new music stands at a cost of $300. The existing ones were imbalanced or broken, and students would often find their sheet music on the floor when practicing. The ribbon-cutting event for the studio was lackluster, and engagement was low. Some faculty didn't even show up. The leadership expressed frustration with the lack of gratitude. Neither group shared their dissatisfaction with the other, and over the course of the following year, that seed of anger grew. The nontenured high performers sought out new opportunities, and the faculty lost talent. If staff had been given a say in how the budget was allocated, the team might still be intact for just $300.

Maslach shared a story with me of a CEO who decided to put a volleyball court on the roof of his office building. Employees looked up at it and saw how seldom people were using it. It made them cynical because that money could have been going to so many other things: "They would think, *If only I had some of that budget, I could fix [insert problem to be solved here]."*

Leaders could save themselves a huge amount of employee stress and subsequent burnout if they were just better at asking people what they need.

Ask Better Questions

When investing in burnout prevention strategies, it's best to narrow down the efforts to small, micro-pilots, which mean a lower budget and less risk. I suggest starting with one or two departments or teams and asking one simple question: If we had this much budget and could spend it on X many items in our department, what would be the first priority? Have the team vote anonymously and then share the data with everyone. Discuss what was prioritized and why and start working down the list. Employees may not have the perfect silver-bullet solution, but they can most certainly tell us what isn't working—and that is often the most invaluable data.

A larger pilot can start with some critical but some simple tactics. For example, take a referendum on some of the annual events. Ask your employees if they like the holiday party or the annual picnic? What would they keep? What would they change? Or is there something else that they would rather do with that money? Digital tools and simple surveys are easy to use and deploy—particularly if you ask a simple question. The part critical to making this tactic successful is in how the data is used. Before engaging in a practice like this—or any employee survey for that matter—something has to be done with the information. If you ask questions and don't bother with a reply, people begin to get wary and stop answering truthfully, or at all.

If sending out questions digitally doesn't feel right, start by walking around. Some of the best data gathering comes from the MBWA style of leadership—management by wandering around. Maslach says she's witnessed hospital CEOs walking the floor, only to realize why people keep asking for, say, a new printer. They see that because the existing one is always breaking down and never serviced, it rarely has paper. So when someone wants to print out something for a patient, they are forced to run down the hall and get somebody to help or to find a printer that works. It's hard for leadership to then ignore needs after witnessing them firsthand.

Organizations have a chance, right now, to fix this type of thing. Burnout is preventable. It requires good organizational hygiene, better data, asking more timely and relevant questions, smarter (more micro) budgeting, and ensuring that wellness offerings are included as part of your well-being strategy. Keep the yoga, the resilience training, and the mindfulness classes—they are all terrific tools for optimizing mental health and managing stress. But, when it comes to employee burnout, remember, it's on you leaders, not them.

———

Jennifer Moss is an award-winning journalist, author, and international public speaker. She is a CBC Radio Columnist, reporting on topics related to happiness and well-being. She contributes regularly to *Harvard Business Review* and writes for the Society of Human Resource Management (SHRM). She sits on the Global Happiness Council in support of the UN's Sustainable Development Goals related to well-being. Her book *Unlocking Happiness at Work* was named Business Book of the Year and her forthcoming book on burnout will be published by Harvard Business Review Press.

NOTE

1. Ben Wigert and Sangeeta Agrawal, "Employee Burnout, Part 1: The Five Main Causes," Gallup, July 12, 2018, https://www.gallup.com/workplace/237059/employee-burnout-part-main-causes.aspx.

CHAPTER 21

Just Hire Better Bosses

by Tomas Chamorro-Premuzic

When it comes to working conditions, we've come a long way in the past 100 years—and not just in the wealthiest countries. Yes, there are still ghastly sweatshops, windowless call centers, and asbestos-ridden factories. But, for the most part, there has arguably never been a better time in history to be employed.

In this industrialized world, most employees desire consumer-like experiences. Stable jobs that pay well and give recognition are no longer enough. People want meaning and purpose, a sense of calling, and jobs that are crafted to their unique personalities. They want

---

Adapted from "To Prevent Burnout, Hire Better Bosses," on hbr.org, August 23, 2019 (product #H054LV).

flexibility, fair compensation, tasks that stimulate, and perhaps most of all, they want to feel safe showing their authentic selves. Top employers know that they must cater to these significant expectations to be serious competitors in the war for talent.

Yet, there's still one, big unaddressed issue that keeps popping up: burnout. In the U.S. alone, workplace stress costs the economy around $300 billion per year in absenteeism, diminished productivity, and legal and medical fees.[1] Unsurprisingly, study after study shows that stress and burnout are major drivers of staff turnover, accidents, injuries, and substance abuse. Even among the top companies and the most desirable places to work, this is a problem—and it's generally the consequence of one thing: bad leadership.

In theory, leaders should be shielding their followers and subordinates from stress, operating as a beacon of calmness and safety throughout difficult times. In reality, however, leaders are more likely to cause stress than to reduce it. Millions of employees around the world suffer the consequences of bad leadership, including burnout, alienation, and decreased mental and physical well-being. This is particularly true when managers practice abusive behaviors, but at times, it's their sheer incompetence that demotivates, demoralizes, and stresses out their teams. Lacking technical expertise, having no clue how to give or receive feedback, failing to understand potential, or a general inability to evaluate their subordinates' performance are just some of the common signs of incompetence.

If organizations want to improve their employees' work experience, they should start by improving their leadership. This will probably do more to reduce workplace stress than any other single measure. To that end, here are four critical lessons you should consider:

Don't Hire Bad Leaders in the First Place

We are better at predicting our behavior than changing it, and that also applies to our leadership problems. While organizations spend much more time and money on leadership development than selection, it should be the other way around. Studies show that leaders' performance—including their tendency to stress employees out—can often be predicted using science-based assessments and data. There is no excuse for hiring leaders who consistently terrorize or alienate their teams. Moreover, it is not easy to simply coach someone to be pleasant, fair, and caring if they do not already attain at least some of those assets naturally.

Organizations should spend more time scrutinizing candidates who apply for leadership roles. Focus less on their past performance (particularly if they are being promoted from an individual contributor role), and more on their actual potential. Do they have the right expertise? Are they curious, smart, and fast learners? Above all, do they have EQ, empathy, and integrity? Using science-based assessments to measure these traits will help companies avoid future leadership problems.

It Is More Profitable to Remove Toxic Leaders Than to Hire Superstars

As a Harvard Business School study shows, it is about twice as profitable for organizations to eliminate parasitic, toxic leaders than to hire top-performing ones.[2] Toxicity spreads faster and more widely than good behavior, and when bad behavior comes from the very top, it can pollute the company culture like a virus.

Organizations can avoid this common trap by not only focusing on leaders' strengths, but also taking into account their potential flaws. What are their toxic or extreme tendencies? Do they display any dark-side traits? The key implication of the research here is that companies will be better off with above-average talent that is well behaved than with badly behaved superstars.

Resilience Can Hide the Effects of Bad Leadership

Few competencies have been in such great demand recently as resilience, perhaps because resilience enables employees to put up with bad managers (same goes for grit). In a similar vein, incompetent leaders can hide their incompetence by hiring resilient employees with high levels of emotional intelligence, as they will show up as "engaged" in employee engagement surveys even when they are poorly managed or unfairly treated.

Organizations therefore need to ensure they don't assemble a workforce that is overly high in EQ or emotional stability. If you mostly recruit people who are dispositionally happy and cheerful as opposed to analytical and honest, it will be harder for you to detect problems with your leadership. Sure, this profile will generally be associated with higher levels of well-being, but it will also mask underlying leadership issues that need to be fixed. It is a bit like only reading customer reviews from your most lenient, positive, and friendly customers: Just because they are polite or have low standards doesn't mean you are doing a great job.

Boring Is Often Better

Although people can stress out (and freak out) for multiple reasons, the most common one is an inability to predict what comes next. Uncertainty is one of the most common drivers of stress. This also applies to leaders, which is why boring managers will be far less likely to stress out their teams and subordinates than managers who are flamboyant, eccentric, or charismatic—especially if they are explosive and unpredictable.

To start, companies can reduce their reliance on short-term interactions, such as the job interview, when gauging leadership potential. The ability to put on a good show or performance during such instances says very little about the ability to be an effective leader. Instead, look into each candidate's track record and references to learn more about their leadership style and character.

If companies are really interested in boosting their workforce's well-being, they should spend less time and money worrying about perks like office layout, team off-sites, and organic snacks, and more time ensuring that their employees are not traumatized by toxic or medio-cre leaders. To provide a stress-free work environment, they need to hire competent leaders. Finding the right person may take more time, but the payoff will be worth the investment—for employees and for the organization at large.

———————

Tomas Chamorro-Premuzic is the chief talent scientist at ManpowerGroup, a professor of business psychology at University College London and at Columbia University, and an associate at Harvard's Entrepreneurial Finance Lab. He is the author of *Why Do So Many Incompetent Men Become Leaders? (and How to Fix It)*, upon which his TEDx talk was based. Follow him on Twitter @drtcp or at www.drtomas.com.

NOTES

1. American Institute of Stress, "Workplace Stress: Are You Experiencing Workplace Stress," survey, https://www.stress.org/workplace-stress.

2. Michael Housman and Dylan Minor, "Toxic Workers," working paper 16-057, Harvard Business School, Boston, 2015.

CHAPTER 22

The Best Ways Your Organization Can Support Working Parents

by Daisy Dowling

Stress and the resulting high risk of burnout among working parents hasn't exactly been a secret—a 2018 study by BPI Network found that 63% of U.S. working parents had experienced burnout—and some well-resourced companies, pre-Covid, offered a buffet of creative and luxurious perks to working parents to help them avoid it.[1] You read about them: things like

Adapted from content posted on hbr.org, January 31, 2017 (product #H03FH7).

unlimited leave, executive coaches for new mothers, food takeout vouchers, and "flying nannies" who join their executive employees on business trips. In their efforts to do the right thing and woo talent, organizations reached for headline-grabbing solutions. But we're in a different normal now—where the struggles of working parents are even more apparent and resources even tighter. So if your organization *can't* offer glossy, cutting-edge benefits, here's what you can do instead.

The most powerful work-life solutions are ones every organization can implement. They're low intervention and low drama. Managers can spearhead many of them, even without institutional backing. And none of them cost an incremental dime.

Over the past decade of leading human-capital and work-life efforts at *Fortune* 500 companies, I've advised management teams and coached individuals struggling to balance the competing demands of work and home. I've experienced the problem firsthand as a busy working mother, too. The following approaches are what I've found the most effective. They may not be glamorous, but they're practical, actionable, and get results.

Start with the facts

Before launching any support programs for working parents, gather the relevant data: Where do parents sit within the organization? What are their attrition patterns? What information can you gather from annual performance reviews or culture-survey data—or simply from informal conversations? The answers, which should be the basis of your working parent programming, may surprise you. One professional services firm I've worked with examined its new-parent retention rates. It didn't find attrition immediately after maternity leave, but there was a previously unseen pattern of departures 12–18 months afterward. The firm's strategy: Hold preemptive manager and HR checkpoints 9 to 12 months afterward, using the time to discuss work-life issues and career path. The result: better relationships between employees and managers, and a significant reduction in turnover. Finding the actual pain point, as opposed to the perceived or assumed one, is what leads to effective solutions.

Define the demographic

Most companies concentrate their efforts on "visible working parents"—for example, new biological mothers—focusing all programming on lactation rooms and other relevant supports. While these are positive, laudable steps, they address the problem too narrowly. Working parenthood is an 18-year job, and it is done by both men and women, biological and adoptive, gay and straight, in all kinds of family structures. Aligning your organization's programs to this reality—for example, by encouraging all employees to use existing personal days for family care needs—better targets the issue in its broad-spectrum reality, and it sends a more inclusive message, too.

Acknowledge and foster peer-to-peer learning

When working parents need advice or motivation, they turn to the real experts: their respected colleagues and mentors, people they trust who understand the politics and culture inside the organization. Providing basic guidance, even simple talking points, to these internal "peer coaches" enables them to deliver the right messages when it matters.

Become a market maker

Leverage your organization's existing infrastructure to connect working parents and to make practical aspects of parenting easier. Goldman Sachs's "Help at Home" intranet bulletin board allows any employee to trade tips and leads on childcare. Other companies use the same platform to let employees pass hand-me-down baby and child products to their colleagues. No intranet? A peg board in the cafeteria works just as well. The result: a more collaborative culture, and employees who spend less time worrying about and solving practical parenting problems.

Focus the resources you do have on key transition points

As in an Olympic relay race, working parenthood depends on the ability to successfully navigate transition points—the handoffs, the turns. Coming back from leave, welcoming a second or third child, or accepting a change in role or schedule are just a few of the transition points that can derail or strain the most competent working-parent employee. That's why concentrating benefits and programming on these critical points can yield significant return on investment. Johnson & Johnson permits mothers and fathers to use their parental leave on a phase-back basis, ensuring not only time out of office but also a gentler return transition. As Peter Fasolo, global head of HR, states: The company doesn't "dictate how someone should slice up those weeks" of leave. Other organizations offer counseling and support for parent employees who are changing roles or moving to a new office or region. Easing these pivot points can keep your employees more focused and engaged in the moment—and over the long haul.

Categorize communications

Mitigate work-life strain and an "always on" culture by categorizing communications, particularly ones sent outside business hours. One top manager I've worked with sends each email with a header: "Not urgent"; "For Monday"; "FYI only"; "Urgent!" These simple labels let her large team, most of whom are working parents, easily sort through what needs to be done ASAP and what can wait until after the ballet recital or the weekend. Encouraging senior managers to do the same can make a huge impact in overall work-life balance perception, with no change in productivity.

Make vacation nonnegotiable

Has every one of your people taken their allotted vacation in the past year? Does anyone have significant accumulated rollover days? Who—and why? How many of them are working parents? Type A professionals working in high-performance organizations often, even in the absence of direct pressure to do so, voluntarily bypass holidays and time off. Among working parents, this practice is particularly dangerous, leading to burnout, family issues, performance decline, or attrition. Smart companies and managers develop ways to signal to their employees that it's time to take a break. At one of my former employers, a demanding professional services firm, division heads left voicemails each June, encouraging their people to plan summer holidays. Another organization I know includes "vacation days taken" at the top of each employee's performance review, prompting manager attention. Encouraging employees to draw down on existing benefits is easier and more powerful than adding additional work-life programs.

Set a visible example

No program or policy will be as effective in supporting and motivating working parent employees as the example of admired leaders who are balancing job and family. The manager who keeps current photos of children at her desk, who visibly leaves early once a month for the school play or soccer game, and who (occasionally) refers to the evening of homework-checking she faces—all while projecting an upbeat, can-do attitude about work—sends a powerful message: I can do this, and you can, too. Make certain you and the other managers in your organization are modeling the behavior and attitudes you want to see in others.

Encourage managers to get personal

Many managers shy away from personal conversation for fear of being inappropriate, and many employees, particularly in pressured environments, hesitate to discuss personal issues for fear of seeming unprofessional or unfocused. Yet in high-performance organizations where hours are long and teams are tight, as one of my coachees puts it, "the job and your life become undistinguishable." Savvy managers can help employees nip many work-life issues in the bud and make their people feel supported simply by opening the door to new conversations—in an appropriate way. At performance review time, asking, "Are there any other career concerns you want to discuss that I may not be aware of?" can effectively open the door. A simple "How were the kids this weekend?" telegraphs your care and lets employees know you have their backs. An employee who feels whole at work is less likely to look for other options.

Advertise resources already in place—and destigmatize their use

Many corporations already have significant employee resources already in place—employee assistance programs, counseling benefits, human resources staffers trained in coaching and employee support. Yet most employees don't know they exist, don't know how to access them, or are certain that access comes with professional consequence. Smart companies make existing benefits visible and accessible to all. For example, GE's "GE for Me" website consolidates all working parent–related support and benefits information in a single, easily navigable location. And as one senior U.S. Navy leader told me, "My job in creating a healthy command climate means advertising the available support—encouraging people to access the practical programs, the counseling." Don't just offer resources—help your people easily reach them.

The personal and organizational challenges of working parenthood are daunting to all of us. But whether you're a sleep-starved new parent, a sympathetic manager, a senior leader, or all of the above, don't fall into the trap of waiting for big changes or of seeing the problem as so big and hairy as to be insurmountable. Find a strategy or approach that works, in the context you work in—and start moving.

Daisy Dowling is the founder and CEO of Workparent, the executive coaching and training firm, and the author of *Workparent: The Complete Guide to Succeeding on the Job, Staying True to Yourself, and Raising Happy Kids* (Harvard Business Review Press, 2021). She can be reached at www.workparent.com.

NOTE

1. "Parental Burnout Crisis in Corporate America," BPI Network, n.d., http://bpinetwork.org/thought-leadership/studies/67.

CHAPTER 23

Employee Burnout Is a Leadership Problem

by Eric Garton

Companies tend to treat employee burnout as a talent management or personal issue rather than a broader organizational challenge. That's a mistake.

The psychological and physical problems of burned-out employees, which cost an estimated $125 billion to $190 billion a year in health-care spending in the U.S., are just the most obvious impacts. The true cost to business can be far greater, thanks to low productivity across organizations, high turnover, and the loss of the most

Adapted from "Employee Burnout Is a Problem with the Company, Not the Person," on hbr.org, April 6, 2017 (product #H03L3U).

capable talent. Executives need to own up to their role in creating the workplace stress that leads to burnout—heavy workloads, job insecurity, and frustrating work routines that include too many meetings and far too little time for creative work. Once executives confront the problem at an organizational level, they can use organizational measures to address it.

In the book I coauthored with Michael C. Mankins, *Time, Talent and Energy*, we note that when employees aren't as productive as they could be, it's usually the organization, not its employees, that is to blame. The same is true for employee burnout. When we looked inside companies with high burnout rates, we saw three common culprits: excessive collaboration, weak time management disciplines, and a tendency to overload the most capable with too much work. These forces not only rob employees of time to concentrate on completing complex tasks or for idea generation, but also crunch the downtime that is necessary for restoration. Here's how leaders can address them.

Excessive Collaboration

Excessive collaboration is a common ailment in organizations with too many decision makers and too many decision-making nodes. It manifests itself in endless rounds of meetings and conference calls to ensure that every stakeholder is heard and aligned. Many corporate cultures require collaboration far beyond what is needed to get the job done. Together, these structural and cultural factors lead to fragmented calendars and even fragmented hours during the day. Our research found that senior executives now receive 200 or more emails per day. The average frontline supervisor devotes about eight hours each week (a full business day) to sending, reading, and answering e-communications—many of which shouldn't have been sent to or answered by those managers.

Burnout is also driven by the always-on digital workplace, too many priorities, and the expectation that employees can use their digital tools to multitask and power through their workloads. Multitasking turns out to be exhausting and counterproductive as we switch back and forth between tasks. The costs of context switching are well documented: Switching to a new task while still in the middle of another increases the time it takes you to finish both tasks by 25%. A Microsoft study found that it takes people an average of 15 minutes to return to an important project after an email interruption.[1]

Companies can begin to address the collaboration overload problem by adjusting organizational structures and routines. One easy step is to look at the number of nodes in the organization. These are intersections in the organizational matrix where a decision maker sits. A proliferation of nodes is a sign of unnecessary organizational complexity, and nodes act as organizational speed bumps, slowing down the action and stealing organizational time and energy.

Companies can also systematically examine how people go about their work. You can, for example, zero-base meeting calendars to determine which meetings are really necessary, how frequently they should be scheduled, how long they last, and who really needs to attend. You can also look at how you staff teams. Instead of isolating star players by distributing them across teams, companies can often get better results by putting the high-energy, high-achieving players together on the same squad and having them tackle the highest-priority work.

In addition to formal organizational changes, leaders can reduce burnout and raise enterprise productivity through softer interventions. For example, by adopting agile principles, leaders can motivate and energize teams, and give individual team members a way to own the results. With agile approaches, teams focus on fewer, more critical activities. Initiative backlogs are used to set priorities, and the team reprioritizes the list whenever they add new tasks. This provides a mechanism for sustained focus on the most important priorities and constant pruning of less important ones. Projects are time-boxed and focused so that there is more doing and less energy-draining process.

Executives can also work on culture and coaching. Leaders can help establish new cultural norms around time and make clear that everyone's time is a precious resource.

Weak Time-Management Disciplines

In most large organizations, the demand for collaboration has significantly outpaced the development of tools, disciplines, and organizational norms to manage it. Most often, employees are left on their own to figure out how to manage their time in ways that will reduce stress and burnout. They have limited ability to fight a corporate culture in which overwork is the norm and even celebrated. And few employees have the power—or temerity—to call off unnecessary meetings.

But company leaders can do something. The first step is to get a handle on the problem. While executives like to measure the benefits of collaboration, few have measured the costs. But there are useful tools to measure how employee time is spent and how that affects burnout and organizational productivity. Ryan Fuller, the cofounder of a workplace analytics startup acquired by Microsoft, notes that executives often simply do not know how much time employees spend on activities that contribute to enterprise productivity, nor do they know how much time is lost or spent on less productive activities. His company's product is now marketed as Microsoft Workplace Analytics and provides one way to estimate how employee time is spent.

Using data from such tools, you can map the places in your organizations where too much time is spent in meetings, emails, or online collaboration. With this information, you can target changes in specific groups and functions to reduce the organizational drag that drains productivity and leads to burnout. Our data suggests that most executives have an opportunity to liberate at least 20% of their employees' time by bringing greater discipline to time management. Equally important, doing so returns to employees control over their calendars. We find that one of the greatest sources of organizational energy is giving employees a sense of autonomy. It pays to give people control of their days. It also helps to avoid micromanaging, which is another contributor to stress.

Overloading of the Most Capable

Employee workloads have increased in many organizations in which hiring has not matched growth; companies overestimate how much can be accomplished with digital productivity tools and rarely check to see if their assumptions are correct. The overload problem is compounded for companies because the best people are the ones whose knowledge is most in demand and who are often the biggest victims of collaboration overload. In one company we studied, the *average* manager was losing one day a week to email and other electronic communications and two days a week to meetings. The *highly talented* managers will lose even more time to collaboration as their overwork earns them more responsibility and an even larger workload.

The same workplace analytic tools that can measure how much employee time is lost to unproductive activities can also measure the excess demands on the time of the best managers, enabling their bosses to redesign workflows or take other steps to avoid overload and burnout.

Everyone knows the human toll of burnout. Unchecked organizational norms insidiously create the conditions for burnout, but leaders can change them to make burnout less likely. Giving people the time to do work that drives the company's success will pay huge dividends by raising productivity, increasing productive output and reducing burnout. Everybody wins.

———————

Eric Garton is a partner in Bain & Company's Chicago office and leader of the firm's Global Organization practice. He is coauthor of *Time, Talent, Energy: Overcome Organizational Drag and Unleash Your Team's Productive Power* (HBR Press, March 2017).

NOTE

1. Travis Bradberry, "How Being Busy Makes You Less Productive," LinkedIn, October 20, 2015, https://www.linkedin.com/pulse/how -being-busy-makes-you-less-productive-dr-travis-bradberry/.

CHAPTER 24

Burnout: What It Is and How to Measure It

by Christina Maslach and Michael P. Leiter

Over the past few years, it has been widely reported that burnout is rampant and growing throughout the world, with alarming statements like "50% of physicians are burned out," or "millennials are now the burnout generation." Burnout is seen as a major problem for many people, and the strong implication is that it is getting worse. However, the phenomenon of burnout is not new—people who have been worn out and turned off by the work they do have appeared in both fictional and nonfictional writing for centuries. In the past 60 years, the term "burnout" has become a popular way of describing this particular phenomenon—for example, the novel entitled *A Burnt-Out Case* in 1960 and the "burnout shops" of the burgeoning tech industries in the 1970s. The vivid imagery associated with the word is a major reason for this popularity, evoking both external threats (a raging fire that destroys everything in its path) and internal response (the flame of personal passion has died out). In time, people started using "burnout" to describe what was going wrong in their own work life.

By the late 1970s, questions were crystallizing: What is the burnout experience? Why is it a problem? What causes it? Answering these questions would require research tools that did not yet exist, which led to the creation of the Maslach Burnout Inventory (MBI). First published in 1981 and now in its fourth edition, the MBI is the first scientifically developed measure of burnout and is used widely in research studies around the world.[1]

More recently the MBI has been applied for other purposes, such as individual diagnosis or organizational metrics. When used correctly, these applications of the MBI can greatly benefit employees and organizations. When used incorrectly, it can result in more confusion about what burnout is rather than greater understanding. Some of these applications are even unethical.

With burnout on the tip of everyone's tongue, we felt it was the right time to assess the use of the MBI in organizations. This chapter will give an overview about what the MBI is, cover some concerning ways that it is being misused, and show how employers should use it for the benefit of employees, organizations, and the world's understanding of burnout.

What Is the MBI?

Based on an extensive body of international research evidence, in May 2019 the World Health Organization made the following statement:

> *Burn-out is . . . an occupational phenomenon. It is **not** classified as a medical condition.*
>
> *Burn-out is a syndrome conceptualized as resulting from chronic workplace stress that has not been successfully managed. It is characterized by three dimensions:*
> - *feelings of energy depletion or exhaustion;*
> - *increased mental distance from one's job, or feelings of negativism or cynicism related to one's job; and*
> - *reduced professional efficacy.*

Burnout is now clearly defined and officially recognized as a legitimate occupational experience that organizations need to address.

The MBI assesses each of these three dimensions of burnout separately. Its format emerged from prior exploratory work on burnout in the 1970s, which used interviews with workers in various health and human service professions, on-site observations of the workplace, and case studies. A number of consistent themes appeared in the form of statements about personal feelings or attitudes (for example, "I feel emotionally drained from my work"), so a series of these statements became the items in the MBI measure. The MBI developed an approach based on the *frequency* with which people experienced those feelings, with responses ranging from "never" to "every day."

After rigorous testing, the MBI-Human Services Survey (MBI-HSS) was published, followed by the MBI-Educators Survey (MBI-ES), and then the MBI-General Survey (MBI-GS), which was developed for use with people in any type of occupation. The MBI-GS was tested in several countries, in several languages.

In all versions, the MBI yields three scores for each respondent: exhaustion, cynicism, and professional efficacy. There is a continuum of frequency scores, from more positive to more negative, rather than an arbitrary dividing point between "present" and "absent." A profile of burnout is indicated by more negative scores on *all three* dimensions.

In research studies, the goal has been to study what things are associated with each of the three dimensions. For example, do some types of workplace conditions make it difficult to do the job well (lower professional efficacy) or create work overload (higher exhaustion)? Does the occurrence of burnout begin with exhaustion, which then leads to cynicism and the decline in professional efficacy, or are there other paths to burnout?

Modifications and Misuses of the MBI

The fact that the MBI produces three scores has led to some challenges. This complexity has led some to seek a simpler outcome by modifying the scoring procedure. First, some people have added the three scores together.

The problem with this additive approach is that the same total score can be achieved by very different combinations of the three dimensions. Another misuse has been to consider the three dimensions as "symptoms" of burnout, and to then argue that a negative score on any *one* of these symptoms constitutes burnout. Another oversimplification has been to use only one question to assess each dimension.

Second, some people have decided to use only one of the three dimensions of burnout (usually exhaustion), implicitly proposing a new definition of burnout. In another variation of this focus on exhaustion, some have argued that the correlation with measures of depression (which contain multiple items about exhaustion) mean that burnout is really just depression.

Third, another scoring modification has involved arbitrarily dividing the sample of respondents in half and inaccurately assuming that the half that has more negative scores is burned out, and the other half is not. Some have used the descriptions of the range of scores, which divide the range into thirds (lower, mid-range, upper), as the arbitrary cutoffs for "low, medium, and high burnout." When their study replicates that same range, they inaccurately claim that "a third of the group is highly burned out."

What leads to all these misuses? A major reason for these scoring modifications (and resulting inaccuracies) is that many think of burnout as some sort of medical disease or disability, and they want a single score that can diagnose whether individual employees have this disability or not, yet we never designed the MBI as a tool to diagnose an individual health problem. Indeed, from the beginning, burnout was *not* considered some type of personal illness or disease—a viewpoint that the WHO reiterated in its May 2019 statement. However, many forms of personal therapy or treatment can only occur, or be covered by insurance, if there is an officially recognized diagnosis within the overall health-care system. There has been continuing pressure to define burnout in medical terms to make it fit within that system.

Even more troubling is the misuse of MBI scores to identify (sometimes publicly) people who are "diagnosed" as burned out and who therefore need to be dealt with in some way ("you should seek counseling," "your team needs to shape up," "you should quit if you can't handle the job"). Research studies consider this nonconfidential use of MBI scores within organizations to be unethical. Given that there is no clinical basis for assuming that burnout is a personal disability, and no evidence for established treatments for it, the use of an individual's scores in this way is clearly wrong.

Best Practices for Using the MBI at Work

The MBI was designed for discovery—both of new information that extends our knowledge about burnout and of possible strategies for change. This discovery can also take place when organizations use the MBI for practical studies and planning. When the MBI is used correctly, and in strategic combination with other relevant information, the findings can help leaders design effective ways to build engagement and establish healthier workplaces in which employees will thrive.

First, new research has revealed how to bring together all three MBI dimensions in a comprehensive and meaningful way.[2] This new scoring procedure for the three dimensions generates five profiles of people's work experience:

- **Burnout:** negative scores on exhaustion, cynicism, and professional efficacy

- **Overextended:** strong negative score on exhaustion only

- **Ineffective:** strong negative score on professional efficacy only

- **Disengaged:** strong negative score on cynicism only

- **Engagement:** strong positive scores on exhaustion, cynicism, and professional efficacy

All five of these experiences need to be better understood, not just the two extremes of burnout and engagement. When measured properly, evidence suggests that only 10% to 15% of employees fit the true burnout profile, whereas the engagement profile appears twice as often, at around 30%. That leaves over half of employees as negative in one or two dimensions—not burned out, but perhaps on the pathway there.

When research findings are gathered on how people are reacting to six key components of their workplace culture (workload, control, reward, community, fairness, values—as reflected by scores on the Areas of Worklife Survey, or AWS), each profile shows a very different pattern.[3] For example, the overextended group has just one key problem: workload (high demands and low resources). But the disengaged or ineffective groups seem to have other problems, including fairness in the workplace, or social rewards and recognition. The burnout group has major issues with multiple aspects of the workplace—a pattern that stands in sharp contrast to the "exhaustion-only" overextended group. Any solution that an employer undertakes to improve the work-life experience needs to account for the varying sources of the five different patterns, rather than assuming that one type of solution will fit all.

Second, organizations should not use the MBI in isolation. They should combine its findings with those of other tools to determine the likely causes of the five profiles. A single summary of employees' MBI scores does not provide any useful guidance on why the summary looks like it does, nor does it suggest possible paths to improvement.

For organizations that do not have internal resources to conduct an applied study of employee burnout and engagement, an alternative option is to obtain assessment services from consultants or test publishers. External surveyors can assure confidentiality by acting as intermediaries between employee respondents and management. They often have a greater capacity to generate individual or work group reports. Large organizations do not have one overall profile on these issues: scores vary considerably across organizational units. Important questions include, What is the percentage of each profile within various units of the organization? Is burnout a problem only in certain areas or within certain occupational specialties? The organization can then use such reports to develop optimal policies and practices to effect positive change.

The online surveys for assessing burnout need to include an option for employees to provide their own written comments and suggestions. People often put a lot of thought and effort into their comments, and the results can give valuable insights, especially if themes emerge across a wide range of responses. Employers may add supplemental questions to target issues that are specific to the organization at that time.

There is an important caveat with respect to these kinds of organizational assessments—*organizations must share the results with the people who generated them.* All too often, we have seen leaders collect information from their employees but never provide any feedback about what they learned and whether they will actually use that information for positive improvements. When employees do work that is not acknowledged, the risk of cynicism and frustration rises. It is important for leaders to reflect on the implications of the pattern of scores and the themes of the comments. Management at all levels has to clearly communicate the importance of the organizational assessment; the goal is to make positive change, and management will take action.

Conclusion

"Burnout" has become a popular umbrella term for whatever distresses people in their work, but we hope that this chapter helps clear up some misconceptions. Although the label can be misused and misunderstood, it is an important red-flag warning that things can go wrong for employees on the job. That warning should not be ignored or downplayed but should incite course corrections. All stakeholders from line workers to the boardroom need a complete understanding of what burnout is and how it can be properly identified and successfully managed; this is essential to reshaping today's workplaces and designing better ones in the future.

———————

Christina Maslach is a professor of psychology and a core researcher at the Healthy Workplaces Center at the University of California, Berkeley. She is the pioneer of research on job burnout, producing the standard assessment tool (the Maslach Burnout Inventory, MBI), books, and award-winning articles. She has been honored with multiple awards, including one from the National Academy of Sciences in 2020. **Michael P. Leiter** is a researcher and writer on psychology, focusing on burnout, work engagement, and social relationships at work. Recent initiatives include improving the quality of work life through enhancing civility and respect among colleagues. He has written extensively on these issues based on his research in North America and Australia.

Residing in Nova Scotia, Canada, he is Honorary Professor, Deakin University and Acadia University.

NOTES

1. C. Maslach and S. E. Jackson, "The Measurement of Experienced Burnout," *Journal of Occupational Behavior* 2 (1981): 99–113. The MBI is a copyrighted measure published and distributed by Mind Garden, a publisher of psychological tests: C. Maslach et al., *Maslach Burnout Inventory Manual*, 4th ed. (Menlo Park, CA: Mind Garden Inc., 2017). Complete information about the psychometric development and use of the MBI is contained in the manual.

2. M. P. Leiter and C. Maslach, "Latent Burnout Profiles: A New Approach to Understanding the Burnout Experience," *Burnout Research* 3 (2016): 89–100.

3. M. P. Leiter and C. Maslach, *Areas of Worklife Survey Manual* (Menlo Park, CA: Mind Garden, Inc., 2017).

Index

Notes

Notes

Notes

Notes

Notes

Notes

Notes

Notes

Engage with HBR content the way you want, on any device.

With HBR's new subscription plans, you can access world-renowned **case studies** from Harvard Business School and receive **four free eBooks**. Download and customize prebuilt **slide decks and graphics** from our **Visual Library**. With HBR's archive, top 50 best-selling articles, and five new articles every day, HBR is more than just a magazine.

Subscribe Today
hbr.org/success

Smart advice and inspiration from a source you trust.

If you enjoyed this book and want more comprehensive guidance on essential professional skills, turn to the HBR Guides Boxed Set. Packed with the practical advice you need to succeed, this seven-volume collection provides smart answers to your most pressing work challenges, from writing more effective emails and delivering persuasive presentations to setting priorities and managing up and across.